Meet Marvis Frazier

The Story of the Son of Smokin' Joe

By Jamie Potter and Marvis Frazier

Foreword by Reggie Bullock

Gopher Graphics
Otego, New York

Copyright © 2013 by Jamie Potter and Marvis Frazier

All rights reserved. No part of this book may be reproduced or transmitted in any form or by any means, electronic or mechanical, including photocopying, recording or by any information storage and retrieval system, without written permission from the publisher, except for the inclusion of brief quotations in a review.

Published 2013

Printed in the United Stated of America

ISBN-13: 978-0-9890924-2-5

Dust Cover Photography by Webster Riddick

Unattributed quotations are the words or thoughts of Marvis Frazier.

10 9 8 7 6 5 4 3 2 1

Published by Gopher Graphics
3883 State Hwy. 7
Otego, New York 13825
607 643 7212
gophergraphics@hotmail.com

With Love ...

When Marvis and I discussed the dedication of this book, our talk went immediately to our dads. After all, Marvis and I are both poppa's boys, so to speak. We both loved, admired, even revered our fathers and considered them remarkable men. Joe Frazier, as everyone knows, was one of the greatest heavyweight boxers of all time, yet he was kind to his fans and loving to his children despite his celebrity status. Joe Frazier was a true gentleman. Jim Potter, although not famous, was a great athlete in his own right. He starred in four sports in high school, once had a tryout with a major league baseball team, and shot golf like a pro. Still, Jim also cared about doing right and raising his family responsibly. Jim Potter was a good man. Sadly, both of our fathers are deceased. Joe Frazier died in November of 2011 and my father followed three months later in January of 2012.

Deciding to dedicate this book to our fathers could have been the end of our discussion, except something wasn't right. Being men, it was easy for Marvis and me to relate to our fathers, especially through sports, but when we thought more about who influenced our lives and helped make us the people we are, we realized that we are both momma's boys too. I wouldn't even be helping Marvis to write his life story if it were not for my mom's creative influences and where do you think that gentle, sensitive part of Marvis Frazier comes from? Therefore, Marvis and I also dedicate this book to our wonderful mothers, who both did what was required of them to raise their children right. Florence Frazier and

Shirley Ingraham showered their children with love, fought for their families when necessary, and provided us all with good examples.

To our fathers, and our mothers, with love... Now we have given credit where credit is due.

Joe and Florence Frazier (Photo courtesy of Darryl Lee)

Jim Potter and Shirley (Potter) Ingraham (Photo from Family Collection)

Acknowledgments

Marvis and Jamie would like to extend special thanks to:

Jenny Bartlett: Our copy editor for the book, who rushed everything through for us despite her own busy schedule as an English teacher and drama director.

Reggie Bullock: We met Reggie when he interviewed Marvis on his radio show. He liked Marvis, we liked Reggie and he ended up writing the foreword for the book.

JoAnn Chmielowski: An artist, musician, and writer who penned a beautiful description of her feelings about the loss of her father which she thoughtfully let us use in the book.

Val Colbert and his wife Elaine Wallace-Colbert: Val is in the book as one of Marvis's trainers but he and his wife Elaine have also been instrumental in its writing, with advice, pictures, and commentary.

George "Doc" Day: The parts of the book that deal with Marvis's injuries and illnesses could not have been written without the assistance of this very knowledgeable registered nurse and long time friend.

Ron Erwin: Thanks to Ron for his excellent reconstructive drawing of Marvis's vision of The Frazier Center, especially considering we didn't give him much to work with.

Dr. Joseph A. Fabiani: As the orthopedist for both Marvis and his father, Dr. Fabiani always found a way to get them back in the ring healthy. He also did a good job telling us how he did it.

Brian Foley: As our website "manager," Brian always has solutions that seem like magic to us, which makes sense considering Brian is also a professional magician (and mathematician)!

Darryl Lee: A friend of the Frazier family for nearly fifty years with a photographic eye and a willingness to share his great picture collection!

Steven Mayisela: Steven is a friend of Jamie's from South Africa who has been an inspiration to him throughout the telling of this story. For that Jamie hopes to tell the story of Steven Mayisela next.

Janet Powers: Jamie's wife who has been absolutely indispensable in using her writing skills to make everything Jamie has written readable.

Jack and Sadie: Jamie's children who patiently listened to him read each of the chapters aloud, sometimes even before their mother had a chance to perform her magic (see above).

Webster Riddick: The incredible Philadelphia sports photographer and long time friend of the Fraziers who provided many of the photographs used in the book.

Dr. Frederick Simeone: Dr. Simeone is the neurosurgeon who performed the operation on Marvis's neck. His description of the injury and the surgery necessary to correct it were crucial to the book.

Foreword

It was March 8, 1971. I was a young boy growing up in the Bronx, New York. Everyone in my neighborhood was rooting for Muhammad Ali to defeat Joe Frazier in the most anticipated sporting event in history. The next day I went to school, sad over the fact that Smokin' Joe Frazier had beaten my hero, Muhammad Ali. It was one of my most painful childhood memories.

About a month after the fight, I saw heavyweight champion Joe Frazier being interviewed on TV. During this interview I noticed that Joe had a son named Marvis, who appeared to be about my age. Seeing Marvis next to his father on TV made me wonder what it would be like to have my father win the biggest event in sports history. My dad was bigger than life to me, a very strong man and hard worker who always provided for his family. Marvis's dad was the same, except he could out-box any man on the planet.

Fast forward about twelve years. My fascination with Marvis Frazier went through the roof when he, like his father before him, fought for the heavyweight championship of the world, battling the undefeated Larry Holmes. It was during this fight that I really connected with Marvis Frazier. I had always felt pressure to live up to my dad's accomplishments, but that pressure was nothing compared to what Marvis must have felt. What was it like to be Marvis Frazier? What was it like to live in the shadow of one of the greatest American sports heroes of all time? Often we think we know the lives of athletes and entertainers, but our knowledge of them is only surface deep. We don't know their hidden pain or joy. We don't know their hidden failures or triumphs. The reality is, until we meet a person, we know very little about them - and I wanted to know every detail of Marvis Frazier's life.

Fast forward thirty more years. I finally get a chance to meet Marvis Frazier. After learning that a book about his life was in the works, I pursued and was able to land a telephone interview with Marvis on my radio show. During that interview, I discovered a fascinating man who is funny (boy is he funny), down to earth, and humble. That interview also led to the opportunity for my thirteen year old son, Isaiah, and me to meet Marvis Frazier for lunch. We were both amazed at this man. I was pleased at how much attention Marvis paid to my son, whom he entertained with delicious stories about boxing, heavily seasoned with life lessons about (among other things) respecting your parents and always making honorable choices. We also got to hear many details of Marvis Frazier's interesting and inspiring life. We learned that Marvis could fight; he was a good boxer. But it is clear that his legacy will be his magnetic personality and his great compassion for people - traits that make him a great son, a great father, a great brother, and to everyone (like my son and me) fortunate enough to meet Marvis Frazier, a great friend!

-Reggie Bullock

Filmmaker and Radio Personality, Reggie Bullock and his son, Isaiah, Meet Marvis Frazier, Christmas time, 2012

CONTENTS

Part I Boxing

Chapter 1
The Warrior Challenges the Chief 19

Chapter 2
Before Larry Holmes: The A-Grade Person 31

Chapter 3
Before Larry Holmes: The Amateur Whiz Kid 43

Chapter 4
Before Larry Holmes: The Undefeated Professional 55

Chapter 5
After Larry Holmes: Two Strikes, but not Out 77

Chapter 6
Wounded Warrior 93

Chapter 7
Mike Who? 103

Chapter 8
Retirement 109

Part II Depression

Chapter 9
It Begins 127

Chapter 10
It Ends 137

Part III Loss

<u>Chapter 11</u>
A Storybook Romance 145

<u>Chapter 12</u>
...with a Sad Ending 161

Part IV Changes

<u>Chapter 13</u>
Life Without Daralyn 173

<u>Chapter 14</u>
A New Dream 179

<u>Chapter 15</u>
Daddy Loves You 187

Part V Hope

<u>Chapter 16</u>
Marvis Frazier Today, a Conversation 197

Afterword
What Meeting Marvis Frazier has meant to me 211

Appendix 1
"Young Christian" by Marvis Frazier 213

Appendix 2
Marvis Frazier's Professional Record and Amateur Awards 215

Appendix 3
Book Writing Outtakes, a Blog Post Record of our Journey 217

Our Photographers 246
Index 247

"You can't cry the blues when you lose, because you're grinning when you're winning."

-Marvis Frazier

(Photo Courtesy of Webster Riddick)

Part I Boxing

"Pop, I messed up so bad."

Chapter 1

The Young Warrior Challenges The Chief

"As I lay on the canvas, all I could think of was - wow, maybe my former trainer Sam Hickman was right when he told me that I wasn't ready to face Larry Holmes."- Marvis Frazier in a 2010 interview.

"Ladies and gentlemen – welcome to tonight's main event – twelve rounds of boxing in the Heavyweight Division. In the Blue corner, fighting out of Philadelphia, Pennsylvania, weighing in at an even two hundred pounds, with a professional record of ten wins, no defeats and six knockouts, here is the undefeated Marvis Frazier! And in the Red corner, from Easton, Pennsylvania, weighing two hundred nineteen pounds, he too is undefeated in his professional career – with forty-four wins, no defeats, thirty one knockouts... the WBC Heavyweight Champion of the World: Larry Holmes!"[1]

The date is November 25th, 1983 - the place, Caesar's Palace in Las Vegas, Nevada. Larry Holmes is the heavyweight champion of the world. He wears the belt of the World Boxing Council and is duly recognized as the champ by anyone who can keep politics out of the ring. Holmes is in pursuit of boxing legend Rocky Marciano's lifetime record. Marciano retired with a record of forty-nine wins with no defeats. Larry Holmes already has

(1) - The words of Las Vegas ring announcer, Chuck Hull

forty-four wins with no defeats. Six more wins without a loss will place him in the ranks of boxing's greats, and at age thirty-four, Holmes would not be frowned upon for getting out of fighting while he is ahead. After all, Marciano retired at age thirty-three and never looked back.

Twenty-three year old Marvis Frazier is also undefeated, but has only ten wins to his credit. His credentials are well earned, however, because he has worked his way up the ranks. In five years as an amateur, he amassed a fantastic fifty-six and two record, including wins over such top notch fighters as Tim Witherspoon, Jimmy Clark, Tony Tubbs, and Mitch Green. Marvis distinguished himself in 1979 by winning the National Golden Gloves Heavyweight Championship and in 1980 with the National Amateur Athletic Union Heavyweight title. As a professional, his short list of victories includes convincing decisions over James Broad and Joe Bugner.

Thus the table is set: youthful zest and courage versus seasoned poise and confidence - The Young Warrior challenges The Chief! This fight involves the heavyweight title held by an undefeated champion and sought after by the son of Smokin' Joe Frazier. The whole world is watching.

The NBC Network is broadcasting in prime time with Ferdie Pacheco and Marv Albert as the on air announcers. It's a packed house at Caesar's Palace. Holmes is surrounded by his usual entourage, and his wife, Diane, is in attendance. For Marvis Frazier, this is his big moment - THE chance for his star to shine...and no one close to him is going to miss it. His entourage includes brothers, cousins, and other members of the Joe Frazier's Gym fight team. In the crowd are many friends and even more

Chapter 1   The Young Warrior Challenges the Chief

family. Family is very important to Marvis, and they are here for him in force. Of course his wife, Daralyn and mother, Florence, his sisters, his brothers, aunts, uncles, and cousins are all in attendance. As for "Pop," Smokin' Joe Frazier himself has the best seat in the house. Joe Frazier is Marvis Frazier's corner man. He is trying to help his son become the second half of boxing's first ever father/son heavyweight champions.

The referee for tonight's fight is Mills Lane. The three knockdown rule is in effect; scoring is on the ten point must system; a fighter cannot be saved by the bell except in the last round; and the standing eight count can be utilized by the referee.

Like the traditional coin toss at the start of a football game, the two fighters come to the middle of the ring and face each other as Mills Lane goes over specific rules and what behavior he will and will not tolerate in the fight. This is a very interesting moment in the fight experience for the astute fan. It is the moment when the fighters use mainly their eyes, but also their body language, their facial expressions, and for some especially brash fighters (to the extent they can get away with it), their words, to send a final message to their opponent before the fight begins. Although the fighters can hear the instructions from the referee, they seem to entirely ignore him as each focuses on the other. Here, Larry Holmes stares unflinchingly at Marvis Frazier, seeming to not even blink. His look seems to say, "I AM THE CHIEF, and everyone knows that! Why are you even daring to challenge me?" Marvis, in response, looks firmly back at Holmes with chin slightly raised. His demeanor seems to answer the look of the Champ with, "I am a Young Warrior, and I am NOT afraid. The end of your reign is at hand!"

Mills Lane finishes his instructions to the fighters. His last words to them are, "Let's get it on!" Larry Holmes and Marvis Frazier return briefly to their respective corners, turn back to face center ring, then with the sound of the bell and a signal from Lane, they come out fighting.

The fight is underway.

Both fighters quickly end up back at center ring. Marvis Frazier throws the first punch. It is a left hook, the punch his father is famous for. It is really more of a lunging left and only hits lightly on the chin of Larry Holmes, who immediately counter punches with a straight right that Marvis ducks.

The two fighters stay at center ring, Frazier dancing and moving with his own version of the bobbing up and down style of his Dad. Holmes follows, watching like a cat, looking for an opportunity to pounce. Both men are feeling each other out, not making any commitments that would open them up or reveal their plan of attack.

Larry Holmes, who has one of the best jabs in the business, begins to fire away. Marvis Frazier, who as an amateur was more successful as a "boxer" than a "slugger," responds with quick movements and solid defense to neutralize Larry's attack.

Holmes—left jab, Marvis—blocks. Holmes—left jab, Marvis blocks. Holmes—left jab, Marvis—blocks. The fighters are circling center ring. Holmes—left jab, Marvis—ducks. Holmes—left jab, Marvis "slips" the punch by moving his head slightly to his left, while Larry's lightning left hand flies past, missing Frazier's chin by less that an inch.

The fighters continue to feel each other out, staying close to that center of the ring. Holmes jabs—Frazier ducks it. Holmes jabs—Frazier slips it. Holmes jabs—Frazier

Chapter 1 The Young Warrior Challenges the Chief

blocks it! More than a dozen punches thrown and not a single solid hit.

Marvis Frazier drops his gloves.

In the sport of boxing, where one punch can end a fight, injure a fighter, end a career, or even kill a man, dropping your gloves in the heat of battle can be very risky, but it sends a message to your opponent. It says in no uncertain terms, "You CANNOT hit me—I am NOT afraid of you!"

Marvis Frazier is dropping his gloves. Marvis Frazier is sending Larry Holmes a message. The Young Warrior is taunting the Chief!

Two minutes and thirty seconds left in this, the very first round, and Larry Holmes rushes toward the "defenseless" Marvis Frazier.

Holmes fires off a succession of lightning fast jabs. Frazier slips one after another, showing great speed himself. Holmes cuts loose a hard overhand right, but Frazier feints quickly to his right, and the Champ's punch again completely misses his agile younger opponent. Now Frazier counters with a surprise overhand left hook that connects! Marvis Frazier is fighting with his gloves at his side. Larry Holmes still can't hit him and as though to rub salt in the wound, Frazier smacks Holmes with a left.

Yet the taunting continues! Marvis Frazier again drops his gloves. Larry Holmes again comes forward. He fires a left jab—Marvis slips it. Holmes fires again—Marvis easily slips it again.

Larry Holmes may be getting frustrated. Almost none of his numerous punches have connected, even with Marvis Frazier's gloves at his side. Holmes throws two more left jabs that Frazier easily avoids. Now Holmes grabs Frazier behind the head with his left glove...and he flings his opponent toward the canvas, in what looks like frustration at his inability to hit Frazier.

Now Marvis Frazier returns to his full fighting stance. Holmes swings a wild left jab that misses and grabs Frazier behind the head again. Now he releases him and throws two more left jabs - both blocked by Marvis.

Marvis pushes a weak right hand punch at the Champ, who counters with another jab. The two fighters are off balance. They collapse into each other. Again Holmes grabs Frazier behind the head, this time with both hands. The taller, stronger Holmes uses this grasp to whip Frazier headlong into the ropes. Referee Mills Lane moves to address the situation, but Marvis rebounds off the ropes back to Holmes at center ring. Lane stops short and the action continues. Holmes goes back to punching: right, left, left - missed, missed, blocked.

And there are two minutes left in the First round.

The two men square off at center ring. Larry Holmes starts again with the jabs, moving deliberately at the challenger, mixing his jabs with an occasional straight right or at times feinting a right and returning quickly with a left. Marvis Frazier keeps moving right and left with both gloves high up to his face, slipping, ducking, and blocking nearly every Holmes punch.

Neither boxer is hurt in the least ... but there - a solid left hook thrown by Frazier hits Holmes flush on the face and knocks the Champion back. Holmes responds by pushing his open left glove into Frazier's face. Frazier tries to move in closer to line up another left hook, but Holmes keeps him at bay with light left jabs that end up as open gloves in Frazier's face. The fighters separate then re-unite with more light jabs, jostling each other. Again the hands of Holmes are in Frazier's face.

Larry shoots a jab and a straight right hand. Marvis

ducks both and comes up with a hard left to the body. That's probably the second hardest punch of the fight so far, and though it might have scored a point with the judges, nobody is hurt.

The Champion continues to fend the challenger off with the open side of his glove in the challenger's face. Frazier at times slaps Holmes' glove away but seems content to keep moving around the center of the ring avoiding the Champion's blows. Here - another slip of the Holmes jab, and there - ducking under a Holmes overhand right.

And there is one minute left in the First Round.

Holmes throws a right hook - Marvis ducks under it.

Holmes throws two left jabs in succession - Marvis blocks both.

Holmes flashes another left jab - Marvis ducks under it and counters with a left hook, grazing the Champion's cheek.

Holmes - left jab, again, another, and again. Marvis - ducks it, slips it, blocks it, and ducks it again, then fires back a left jab of his own.

The round is winding down.

The two men stand at center ring.

The Champion tries again. He starts with the same, the left jab, but this time lower, and now he feints a right. Marvis reacts, dropping his left guard as Larry's left comes in. Now the second time, Holmes throws a lower left jab and feints a right. Marvis reacts the same way as before and drops his left guard.

Larry Holmes sees this. The undefeated heavyweight world champion, veteran of forty-four pro fights, sees this pattern.

Marvis Frazier, also undefeated but only in his eleventh professional fight, does not.

Larry Holmes throws out a lower left jab for the third time.

Marvis Frazier blocks the incoming jab with his right glove, and drops his left guard again.

The Chief plants himself and lets fly an overhand right bomb.

BOOM!

The Young Warrior is down.

That is the kind of punch that can end a fight. A haymaker. A show stopper. Lights out, game over. Marvis Frazier is flat on the canvas, face down. Over in his corner, just outside of the ring, his Dad looks distraught. Mills Lane begins the ten count. Frazier looks finished.

But no ... at the count of two Marvis springs back to life! He is up on one knee facing the referee. At the count of eight he is back on his feet and ready to go on. Mills Lane checks his gloves, and signals the fight to continue. With thirty-eight seconds on the clock, Marvis Frazier heads back toward the Champ. But how badly is he hurt, and does he have the size and experience to survive the round?

Back to center ring Frazier rushes at Holmes, determined to overcome the blow. The fighters nearly collide as Holmes likewise rushes at Frazier to finish him off. Larry wants to end it now at center ring with another big right hand, but Marvis is still dancing and Holmes settles for two more left jabs. Holmes wisely goes to the body - a strong right hand to the ribs, followed by a quick left, right combination to the head.

Twenty-eight seconds to go in the round, and the action continues in the center of the ring.

Now Holmes unloads a barrage of punches, missing with most of them but whipping the crowd into a frenzy. The Young Warrior is wounded but may survive.

Chapter 1 The Young Warrior Challenges the Chief

Twenty-four seconds to go.

Holmes throws another big overhand right. Marvis ducks it, but in doing so reverses his direction. He is now moving counterclockwise, falling out of orbit and moving toward the corner.

Holmes sees the change and the opportunity. He pursues, cutting off any clockwise lane back to center ring.

Eighteen seconds left in the round and Marvis Frazier is in trouble. Larry Holmes has trapped him in the corner, and Marvis isn't big enough to clinch and hold on or strong enough to fight his way out. It's like Frazier is riding a bucking bronco, and he has to stay on for eighteen more seconds. Larry Holmes wants a home run and begins to swing away. Holmes is throwing nearly a punch every second, though only half of them are hitting. Marvis is just hanging on. At fifteen seconds to go, the Champ looks back at referee, Mills Lane, but he gives no response. At thirteen seconds to go, Holmes slams an explosive right to Frazier's head. At eleven seconds to go, Larry looks again to Mills Lane, and again the referee gives no response. Holmes then goes hard to the body. With ten seconds to go, Marvis throws a weak jab. At eight seconds to go, Holmes unloads another right. Frazier looks hurt - and yet, he keeps his gloves up high and blocks the next three shots by the Champ. The seconds keep ticking away.

Then, with only three seconds to go in the round, while Marvis Frazier is still up, still defending himself, still riding that bucking bronco, referee Mills Lane steps in and with waving arms, separates the fighters.

Marvis looks on as the referee gives the signal.

The Chief has turned back the Young Warrior.

Marvis Frazier slowly closes his eyes and drops his head in utter defeat.

The fight is over.

Smokin' Joe Frazier rushes to embrace his son.

Almost twenty-five years later, Marvis would relate, "What I remember most about that fight was when I got knocked down. I could hear Mills Lane counting: one, two ... and I rolled over and got on one knee, and he asked me, 'Are you alright son, are you alright to continue?' I answered, 'Yes sir, I'm alright to continue.' He said 'Okay then let's get it on.' I lost track of how many punches Larry caught me with after that, but Mills Lane stepped in between us and grabbed me and hugged me and said, 'Son, I apologize, but I have to stop the fight.'"

"When he said that to me, I dropped my head down - tears started coming down my cheeks. No man in the world could be any lower than I was at that moment of my life, because I was fighting to bring the Championship of the World back to my family, and I had failed. I wasn't concerned with what the media had to say. I wasn't concerned with what my friends or fans had to say. I wasn't even concerned with what my mother or my wife had to say. The only concern I had was what did Joe Frazier have to say, because I felt I had messed up that bad, and there was no way that Joe Frazier could forgive Marvis Frazier for embarrassing his name in front of the whole world."

"So, I was standing in the ring with tears coming down my cheeks and I could see my father coming through the ropes and walking toward me. I said, 'Pop, I messed up so bad.' But my father walked up to me. He had a big smile on his face, and his arms opened as wide as the world. He hugged me, and he said 'Don't worry son, I've got ya. You're my son, and I love you. Don't worry about what the world says. I love you.' And I love my Dad. My father is the greatest!"

Foes for one fight. (Photo Courtesy of Webster Riddick)

Friends forever. (Photo Courtesy of Webster Riddick)

Chapter 2

Before Larry Holmes: The "A" Grade Person

"(Marvis) thanked me for having him on the (fight) card (that night). He said he hoped I was satisfied with how he performed. Fighters just don't do that sort of thing." Promoter Sam Glass commenting on Marvis Frazier's graciousness.

If Marvis Frazier had managed to capture the heavyweight crown, boxing fans the world over would have had a champion to admire. As an athlete, Marvis was the model of good sportsmanship. In practice, he dedicated himself to the training required to achieve the physical prowess and skills necessary to be a contender. Val Colbert, a trainer and corner man for both Joe and Marvis Frazier, remembers Marvis always arriving at the gym on time or earlier, often staying late, and at times showing up back at the gym the day after a fight. Although Marvis enjoyed the comradery of other gym members during practice and was easy going and fun to be around, his intensity and focus when it really mattered were unsurpassed. In competition, Marvis was a throwback to more civil times. He didn't gloat when he won, and he didn't whine when he lost. During the after fight interviews, Marvis usually gave thanks to his Lord and Savior, Jesus Christ ("because without Him none of this would have been possible for me to do") and then thanked the other boxer for the opportunity to fight him.

As a person, Marvis was a real gem. Finding anyone to disagree with this statement might be nearly impossible, but finding people to verify it is easy. Mort Sharnik of CBS television said, "Marvis is such a gentle man." Boxing promoter Sam Glass called Marvis, "uncommonly gracious." Marvis's dad, Smokin' Joe, called him, "responsible ... polite ... as decent as they come." Neil Leifer, award winning photographer said, "In an age of spoiled brats in sports, Marvis Frazier is a breath of fresh air." Even Larry Holmes called Marvis, "a good kid ... respectful ... and not the least spoiled." Trainer Val Colbert summed it all up when he said, "Marvis is an A-grade person — that's the best."

Of course boxing is a tough sport, filled with tough men. The pathway to the professional level of many sports typically starts with exceptional youth level performance then passes through elite college play. Boxing careers often start with a troubled kid being the most brutal guy in a rough neighborhood. The kid beating everyone else up gets noticed, is somehow convinced to take all that energy to the gym, realizes that fighting might get him somewhere other than a jail cell, and a boxing career is underway. Many of the great fighters in history started this way - George Foreman, Larry Holmes, and Mike Tyson to name a few. Even Rocky Marciano came to consider professional boxing after he and his brother noticed how powerful his punches were in a fight he had at work. Marvis Frazier did not fit this mold. He wasn't a troubled kid. He was a peacemaker. Marvis was the one who tried to stop the fights among playmates and family members. He didn't live in a rough neighborhood. As the heavyweight champion of the world, his father, Smokin'

Joe, had provided very well for his family. Marvis lived in a beautiful home in a nice neighborhood. Sure, Marvis was in his share of fights as a kid, but he was usually on the receiving end. Bullies, or other kids who wanted to make a name for themselves, upon hearing that Marvis was the son of the heavyweight champion, menaced him or attacked him physically. No, Marvis Frazier was not the tough kid turned professional boxing prospect, and the idea of being a professional boxer never really crossed his mind. That desire came much later and for an entirely different reason.

Marvis, like his dad, Joe Frazier, and his mom, Florence Smith, was born in Beaufort County, South Carolina, a place he only called home for two years, but an area he cherished returning to throughout his childhood. He was the oldest and only boy of the five kids in his family. His mom, Florence, chose the unusual name "Marvis" for her first born, because a friend of her cousin had that name, and she liked it. Together, Florence, Marvis, and sister Jacqui followed Joe as he pursued better opportunity to the north. For the first couple of years, that opportunity avoided Joe Frazier as he tried odd jobs while staying with his brother in New York City and working at a slaughterhouse in Philadelphia (remember the movie *Rocky*?). Finally, feeling out of shape and wanting to act on a childhood dream he had of becoming the next Joe Louis, Joe Frazier joined a gym early in 1962. Two years later he won the gold medal at the Olympics, six years later he was the New York Heavyweight Champion, and by 1970 he was the WBA Heavyweight Champion of the world.

While Smokin' Joe was busy fighting his way to the top, son Marvis was getting along just fine. The specter of a famous father was kept under control by a well grounded mother determined to raise her kids normally, despite Joe's mounting fame and eventual fortune. As sisters Jacquelyn, Weatta, Jo-Netta and Natasha came along, Marvis had to take on the role of big brother more and more, and as Dad was often away, that of Man of the House. Marvis took the responsibilities of these roles quite seriously, and in carrying them out his cares and concerns stayed well within the range of normal. Still, having Smokin' Joe Frazier as your father, the winner of an Olympic Gold Medal, and a contender for the heavyweight championship of the world, had it's affect on the boy's psyche. This was especially the case when the bigger than life man would arrive home unexpectedly, usually at night after bedtime. His thunderous arrival would belie the warm affection he would bestow upon Marvis and his sisters whom he often invited out to play "monster" on the living room floor. If some disciplinary measure was required for bad behavior displayed while Dad was away, it usually took the form of a threat from a man who could carry it out but didn't have to. Just hearing, "Smell this fist." was enough - no smelling was necessary.

Despite their physical separation necessitated by Joe's career, Marvis developed a deep seated admiration for his dad that would eventually be the magnet that would draw Marvis into boxing.

As a young child, Marvis naturally had no real concept of his father as a boxer by profession, although two vivid memories of those times remain. The first was after Joe had won the Olympic Gold medal as a heavyweight in 1964. During the semifinals in Tokyo, Joe had busted up his left thumb while busting up his opponent, Russian boxer Vadim Yemelayanov. Although he knew it was damaged, Joe kept it a secret so as to not risk being scratched from the finals against Hans Huber of Germany. After winning the gold with a close decision, a full examination of Joe's left thumb revealed that it was dislocated and broken in several places and would require two operations and several months of rehabilitation to properly heal. Marvis, age four, knew nothing of all these events except that Daddy left for Tokyo, Japan (wherever that was) in a big plane and came back with his hand in a cast (and a gold medal around his neck)! However, by Christmas of that year a lifelong memory for young Marvis would be formed.

Despite winning the Olympic Gold Medal, Joe couldn't find the backing he needed to propel him to the professional level. Prospective backers thought he was too small to take on the big heavyweights of his day (the same criticism Marvis would face twenty years later). And the injury Joe had suffered to win that medal had also cost him his job at the slaughterhouse. Here it was almost Christmas and an Olympic hero was struggling. That is, until "Clarence" entered the picture. Except his name was Jack Fried, not Clarence, and he was a newspaper reporter, not an angel. Mr. Fried heard about Joe Frazier's woes and wrote a very appealing story about it in the Philadelphia Bulletin. The story was a big hit and had *"It's a Wonderful Life"* results. Gifts of all kinds flowed in from all over, including money to pay bills. With bills paid and gifts galore, the Frazier family had a very merry Christmas that year - one that four year old Marvis would never forget.

The second memorable event for Marvis during the early years of his dad's career, took place four years later. On March 4th of 1968, Joe knocked out his old Olympic trials nemesis, Buster Mathis, to win the New York heavyweight title. Since Muhammad Ali had been stripped of his title for refusing to be inducted into the armed forces, and the World Boxing Association was busy putting together an elimination tournament to find his successor, the athletic commissions of many states accepted Joe Frazier as the heavyweight champion of the world after this victory. For eight year old Marvis and his sisters Jacquelyn and Weatta, their daddy's recognition as the world champ didn't really mean that much. Not, that is until that strange day at school. An unexpected assembly for all the students had the kids buzzing with excitement, but no one seemed to know what it was for. As the school principal quieted the students, Marvis was startled to hear his name called out. He and his sisters were asked to come to the stage in front of all the other kids! As they nervously moved into place and sat in chairs on the platform, handmade crowns were placed on their heads. Still puzzled, the three sat quietly. Suddenly, the entire student body broke the silence when they roared, "One, two, three, four—who are we for ... JOE FRAZIER!" The surprise assembly was a salute to the new heavyweight champion of the world and an acknowledgment of his three children. "This is Marvis Frazier," the principal had said, "son of world heavyweight champion, Joe Frazier." And as poor Marvis would find out in the days and weeks to come, the principal might just as well have added "So, let the beatings begin!"

Of course, eventually Marvis would have no reason to fear the school bullies, who would pick fights with the son of Joe Frazier just to make a name for themselves. By the time Marvis was fourteen, nature had turned the tall slight build he had as an eight year old into the solid muscular frame of his dad, only taller and better proportioned. This same build was ideal for athletic competition of all sorts. As a junior high school student, Marvis excelled in baseball, football, and wrestling. Especially wrestling which was a sport that Marvis was already regional

Chapter 2   Before Larry Holmes : The "A" Grade Person   37

champion of by the ninth grade. One has to wonder how far Marvis could have gone in any of these sports, but it was not to be. When Marvis turned fifteen, his dad treated him to the birthday celebration of a lifetime ... and another sport had grabbed his attention.

*   *   *

When Smokin' Joe Frazier defeated Muhammad Ali in the "Fight of the Century" in 1971, many people believed that the physical toll of that battle was so high that both fighters would never be the same. Indeed, for Smokin' Joe, a few title defenses in the year and a half after against mediocre opponents, followed by the devastating loss to Big George Foreman in 1973 seemed to verify the conjectures of the experts. Even his January, 1974, rematch with Ali, which Joe lost by decision, added fuel to the fire of the idea that he was finished. Ali's strategy to tie Frazier up throughout the fight helped him win the decision but did little to dispel the belief that he, too, was on the wane. Nevertheless, the events of the rest of 1974 and 1975 would quiet the critics and set the stage for a third and final meeting between these two gladiators. Ali stunned the world when he used his "rope-a-dope," extreme endurance, and incredible boxing skills to destroy "the monster," George Foreman, on October 30th, 1974, in Zaire, knocking him out in the 8th round and regaining the heavyweight title. Joe Frazier, at the same time, was in the background easily defeating two other top contenders. He TKO'd Jerry Quarry in June of 1974, and Jimmy Ellis in March of 1975. By the early fall of 1975, a fight was being planned that seemed like 1971's "Fight of the Century" all over again - Muhammad Ali vs. Joe Frazier for the heavyweight championship of the world. It was the "Thrilla in Manila," and fifteen year old Marvis Frazier would be there.

Actually, when father and son left for the Philippines on September 11th, 1975, Marvis was still only fourteen. When they arrived, after crossing the international dateline, it was September 13th. Sadly, Marvis, whose birthday was on the 12th, had "lost" his fifteenth birthday. But Pop would certainly make it up to him.

This birthday party would last for nearly three weeks; nearly three weeks of no school with Pop's permission; nearly three weeks of experiencing life in another country (the fun and festivities of the Philippines); but most importantly, nearly three weeks of being one of the guys in a boxing camp in final preparation for a heavyweight championship bout.

For Marvis Frazier, the experience in Manilla marked a turning point in his life, a genuine coming of age, and it all started with a song. The Frazier camp had arrived in the Philippines first but with very little fanfare. The arrival of Ali's entourage a few days later was treated as a grand celebration. Marvis was there to join in. He met "Mr. Ali" at the airport and treated him to the singing of the Van McCoy song, *First Round Knock Out*. Ali jested with Marvis as he sang, but Marvis sang on, enjoying this encounter with the Champ, though sincerely warning him about the intentions of his dad, Smokin' Joe, to win this fight.

The next song to be sung was *Happy Birthday to You*. Everybody in the Frazier Camp sang it for Marvis at his fifteenth birthday party, which was attended by Philippines President Marcos and his wife, Imelda. The birthday bash was a big one and included a giant cake topped with two statues of sumo wrestlers squaring off for battle, reminiscent of Marvis's own matches as a junior high school wrestling champion. That party had just about everything, except fireworks. Then again Muhammad Ali provided plenty of those.

Of the three fights between Muhammad Ali and Smokin' Joe Frazier, this was the one that Ali hyped up the most. As soon as the deal was made, Ali cut loose on Frazier, and although this great showman was the best one man promoting machine in the world of sports, during the promotion of this fight, Ali may have crossed the line. Entire books have been written about the relationship between Ali and Frazier, and everyone agrees that by the third meeting it had become a blood feud. Ali pulled one prank after another in Manila but the most outrageous was his showing up in front of the Frazier's hotel waving what appeared to be a loaded gun. It was three-thirty in the morning and although they were nine floors up, Ali got Marvis and Joe's attention by shouting out, "I want Joe Frazier. Where is Joe Frazier?" while waving the pistol. Smokin' Joe walked fearlessly out onto the balcony to see what was up, but Marvis thought that maybe "Mr. Ali" had finally cracked, the gun was real, and this crazed man really meant to shoot his pop. Ali did actually pull the trigger several times but, alas, it was only a toy gun. So much for showmanship! Later, Marvis would have one more encounter with "Mr. Ali" where the tone would be totally different, but first, there was a heavyweight fight to prepare for.

At fifteen, Marvis was big for his age and athletically built. From his participation in school sports, he was familiar with the requirements and regimens necessary to get ready for athletic competition. Therefore, he fit right in with the camp crew as they went through their daily routines. Marvis joined his dad and the sparring partners for the early morning runs and impressed them with his speed and stamina. At the makeshift gym in Manila set up for Joe's training, Marvis participated in boxing practice for the first time in his life. Jumping rope, hitting the heavy bag and the speed bag, even smacking the hand pads, were all things Marvis tried, enjoyed, and did well. One of Smokin' Joe's sparring partners, "Scrap Iron" Johnson, worked with Marvis when "Scrap Iron" wasn't in the ring with Joe and encouraged Marvis with flattering comments about his potential. "Hey, you could do it. You could be the next heavyweight champ!" Johnson would say as he steadied the heavy bag against Marvis's rain of blows. When he wasn't imitating the crew in their training practices, Marvis was helping out any way he could - getting water or fetching needed equipment, and always soaking in everything he was seeing and hearing en route. Soon an idea started to form in this young man's head. Marvis was already an outstanding wrestler and football player in school. Why couldn't he be a boxer too? Sure, he could be the Champ, just like his pop—think of all that money! "Hurry up Marvis, we need those wraps over here now," trainer Georgie Benton would call, snapping him out of his daydreaming, "We've got a fight in a few days!"

And what a fight it was, "The Thrilla in Manila." Muhammad Ali versus Smokin' Joe Frazier for the third and final time. The rubber match to a blood feud, with the heavyweight title again on the line. Many consider this one of the greatest fights of all time, certainly one of the most brutal. "The closest thing you'll ever see to death," Ali would later call it. A worthy battle for two of the greatest fighters of all time, though a sorrowful ending for the Frazier camp when in dramatic fashion, Joe's trainers threw in the towel at the beginning of the fifteenth round. Joe protested vehemently, but Eddie Futch had no desire to witness the death of his man in the ring, so he overruled Joe's pleas to let the fight go on. Legend has it that in equally dramatic fashion, an exhausted Ali was in his corner before the fifteenth round pleading with his trainers to stop the fight, and, indeed, when the fight was stopped by Frazier's corner, Ali collapsed onto the canvas.

For Marvis, who was part of the corner team for his father as the "bucket boy" (keeping the sponges soaked, rinsed, and squeezed out as needed), he witnessed the fight in all its drama first hand. He cheered for and feared for his father. He also felt an unexpected excitement as the drama unfolded. The fleeting thoughts about being a boxer, that Marvis had experienced during practice, were now taking hold. "I really could be a boxer," Marvis thought early in the fight. "I want to be a boxer," Marvis felt in the middle rounds when the fight was so close. "I am going to be a boxer, and I'm going to bring the heavyweight championship of the world back to the Frazier family," Marvis decided as he saw the towel being thrown in by the Frazier corner and was saddened by the realization that Smokin' Joe had failed to regain the title. This was the turning point of his life. This was the coming of age. Marvis was going to be a boxer, just like his pop, and he was sure that someday he would be the heavyweight champion of the world.

After the fight was over, there was one more lesson, one more historical moment for his life from this experience. Muhammad Ali was lying in his locker room calling for Marvis. Despite winning the fight, Ali's locker room was quiet. There lay Ali in agony from the beating he had received from Frazier. In a low hoarse voice Ali spoke to Marvis,

"All those things I said about your father, I apologize. Will you tell that to your father for me?" Marvis paused briefly before answering. "Yes, sir." Marvis responded, humbled and at the same time awestruck by the situation. He took one step back, turned, and left the room.

To his pop, Marvis told "Mr. Ali's" message. Outside of his father's earshot he told everyone else from the Frazier camp that he was going to be a boxer, and he was going to get the title back for the Frazier family! Little did they know that Marvis Frazier was absolutely serious.

The three week long birthday party was nearly over. It was time to break camp and head back to Philadelphia, Pennsylvania, USA. Smokin' Joe was recovering quickly from the ordeal that would prove to be his last hurrah as a serious contender and suggested that they all stop off in Hawaii on their way home. Marvis happily agreed. After all - Hawaii! Plus, back at home he had the return to school waiting for him ... and, there was a decision he had made that he had to tell his father about.

Nearly thirty-five years after his amazing fifteenth birthday experience, Marvis would recall that, "From the time I was little, I loved being a Frazier - not because my father was the heavyweight champion of the world, but because I loved my family. I loved my mom. I loved my pop. I loved my sisters. I loved being a Frazier - being part of the Frazier family. When I first started playing sports in school, I knew I was gifted athletically, winning easily at everything I tried. So, when I decided at the age of fifteen that I was going to become a boxer, I was doing it to return the heavyweight championship to the Frazier family - the family that I loved. And because I excelled in sports, I knew I could do it. This wasn't some passing childhood fantasy. I thought about it all the time. It became my dream. And I began pursuing that dream from the moment the thought entered my head."

Chapter 3

Before Larry Holmes: The Amateur Whiz Kid

"I felt like the King of the world." Marvis Frazier commenting in 2011 on his state of mind at the completion of his amateur career.

Only a few days after arriving back in Philadelphia, Marvis approached his father about becoming a boxer. It was almost like asking a man for his daughter's hand in marriage. Marvis knew he was going to try boxing but his father's blessing would make the experience better. Joe's answer was quick and blunt. "No." Marvis was surprised. Joe continued, "You don't want that, that's too much work." Marvis was shaking his head in disagreement, like youngsters often do. "You can be something else, ANYTHING else! Boxing is hard work. It's a tough sport and a hard life. You should do something easier."

But was Joe's response sincere advice, or was he actually happy to hear of Marvis's wish to box and this was just a cagey way to goad the young man on? After all, boxing was a tough racket, and Joe knew Marvis's desire would have to be tested. Marvis was not deterred. "But, Pop, I really do want to be a boxer." Finally, Joe agreed, with two conditions. "Okay son, you have my permission to try boxing for two weeks. Then, let's see if you still want to be a boxer. But, you have to ask your mother first."

"Oh, you and your father are going to kill me!" Florence Frazier exclaimed when her only son asked if he could try the sport of boxing. "Well, what did your father say? I guess if it's alright with him, then it's alright with me," Florence conceded, giving in to the desire of Marvis to try boxing. She trusted that Joe knew what was best for their son, though as a mother, she was naturally fearful of the punishing nature of the sport on her first born. Ironically, years later her oldest daughter, Jacquelyn, would add to Mrs. Frazier's fears for her family when she, too, would join the fight game.

Compared to asking his mom, Marvis figured the two week trial period was going to be a breeze. Marvis was back at school and still on the wrestling team, so as a fledgling boxer his schedule went something like this: in school from eight in the morning until three in the afternoon, wrestling practice from three-thirty to five, then rushing home for supper, chores, and homework. Then he would take a bus, a trolley, and a three block walk (or run) to get to his dad's gym. After two hours of an intense boxing workout, followed again by three blocks on foot, a trolley, and a bus ride, he'd arrive back at home just in time to fall into bed. Whew! But Marvis loved it, and it didn't take the entire two weeks for Smokin' Joe to see that his son was serious about boxing. With that realization, Joe set out to assign the right trainers for Marvis. This part was easy. Joe Frazier's Gym already had an excellent staff to handle the incoming fighters, and Marvis would be treated just like any other beginning boxer.

Philadelphia is the spiritual home of boxing in the United States, and Joe Frazier's Gym was the heart of that spirit. Located on North Broad Street, close to North Philadelphia's Amtrak station, the gym was opened in the late 1960's by Cloverlay, Inc. This group of investors financed and ran Joe Frazier's career. A few years before

Chapter 3 Before Larry Holmes: The Amateur Whiz Kid

Joe's first fight with Muhammad Ali, Cloverlay bought a three story building at 2917 North Broad and had it converted into a training facility for Smokin' Joe. Frazier himself trained there for the remainder of his career, which resulted in many of the world's best boxers putting in appearances, either to spar with Joe and learn from the master (such as Larry Holmes and Ken Norton did), or just to be where the action was, to be a part of boxing history.

By the time Marvis Frazier began training at his dad's gym, programs were in place to accommodate boxers at all interest levels. Whether for the sake of the good conditioning that a boxing workout affords or the desire to compete in the ring as an amateur or eventually a professional, Joe Frazier's Gym in Philadelphia was the place to make it happen. Not only was the gym swarming with some of the best pugilists on the planet, but the staff included some of the top trainers in the sport. Marvis was fortunate to be under the care of this outstanding staff, but three men in particular were charged with the task of focusing his natural athleticism and exceptional enthusiasm on the sport of boxing. For Marvis and all of the amateurs at Joe Frazier's Gym, it started with Sam Hickman.

For a former Green Beret, Sam Hickman was surprisingly soft-spoken. It was his job to coordinate the matches for the amateur fighters. He was the "scout" or "look out man" for Joe Frazier's Gym. As such, Hickman's judgment of the abilities of his own fighters and amateur fighters throughout the country was crucial in helping to match up boxers who were similarly skilled. The importance of this job in boxing cannot be overstated. Contests between mismatched fighters can result in serious harm to the body or self-confidence of the losing boxer, possibly hampering or ending his career prematurely.

The winner in such contests adds a notch on his belt for the win but gains little from the experience and risks an overinflated self-confidence. To perform this job so expertly, Sam Hickman observed his boxers very closely and for long periods of time. Sam also studied other amateur boxers across the country, many times traveling to see their fights. As the "Look Out Man" for Marvis, Sam was nearly flawless in his job: helping Joe decide when Marvis was ready for his first fight, guiding him through a fifty-six and two amateur career as he rose to become one of the best amateur heavyweight boxers in the world, and finally, helping Joe again to decide when Marvis was ready to begin his professional career.

Sam Hickman may have picked the fights for Marvis, but it was his trainers who prepared him for those fights. The day to day routine of building a boxer, from the workouts to the sparring to the matches themselves fell on the shoulders of trainers George Benton and Val Colbert.

George Benton, a native Philadelphian, was a world class boxer himself, contending for the middleweight title in the 1960's. He posted an overall record of sixty-two wins and thirteen losses, one of those being a 1963 split decision loss to Rubin "Hurricane" Carter. After his retirement in 1970, George put his knowledge to work as a trainer, working with such big name boxers as Joe Frazier, Evander Holyfield, Jimmy Young, and Leon Spinks. George was even elected to the Boxing Hall of Fame as a trainer in 2001. George Benton was especially suited as a trainer for Marvis Frazier. Like Marvis, he was known for his quiet demeanor, and his boxing style fit Marvis to a tee. Marvis was smaller than many of his heavyweight opponents but very quick. George's "The art of boxing is to hit and not get hit" strategy addressed this situation perfectly.

Vellen Colbert was born in Emanuel County, Georgia but had come to Philadelphia to visit a cousin and had stayed. Val befriended George Benton who brought him into the gym as a trainer. Val had done little boxing himself but knew about athletic training from his years as a wrestler. He complimented George nicely because he too was easy going and thoughtful of others. Val's wife, Elaine, tells of the cold winter day when Val showed up with no coat, having given it to a homeless man he saw during his walk home from the gym. Val's training work consisted of following up with procedures that George prescribed for each boxer. Val became very close to Marvis as his career proceeded, basically taking the role of a quiet version of Muhammad Ali's famous corner man Bundini Brown. Val, who had the job of helping Marvis select the "keys" necessary for victory in each of his fights, also helped Marvis in many uplifting ways in his life outside of boxing.

These were the three men whom Joe Frazier entrusted with the amateur career of his son. Joe himself still had his own career to contend with (although it was winding down), as well as his musical career as the lead singer for *"Smokin' Joe and the Knockouts"* and *"The Smokin' Joe Frazier Revue."* Joe was confident, however, that Marvis was in good hands and kept abreast of his progress through contact with George Benton and by occasionally showing up at his son's amateur matches. As it turned out, these three would mold Marvis into a fighter who would take the amateur heavyweight boxing world by storm.

Driven by what rock star Joe Walsh labeled in one of his songs as "the-hurry-up-hunger-of-growing-up," young Marvis Frazier figured that everything would move on a fast track to success in his dream to become the heavyweight champion of the world. However, his father and the training staff at the gym had a different idea. All beginning boxers were required to complete a regimen of conditioning and boxing workouts before they were allowed to step into the ring. For Marvis this phase of training went on for seven long months - but Marvis didn't mind. He kept his nose to the grindstone, determined to prove to his father that he was sincere in his desire to become a boxer. Once the beginners earned their way into the ring, they continued with the conditioning and boxing workouts, while adding sparring with an opponent for a period of time, before they were allowed to box competitively. For Marvis, this second phase of training went on for five more months - but Marvis didn't mind. He was finally in the ring and testing the skills he had learned from George and Val. Because Marvis was training at Joe Frazier's Gym, he had some of the world's best to spar with. One of the first guys Marvis faced was Willie "The Worm" Monroe. Monroe, like George Benton, was a native of Philadelphia. He was a well respected middleweight who was one of only three people to beat Marvin Hagler. At the time Marvis climbed into the ring to spar with Willie, Monroe was still actively pursuing his professional career. It was a great opportunity for Marvis, but Willie "The Worm" Monroe made Marvis pay for the opportunity. He especially liked to hit Marvis in the nose and that he did - often! Marvis would come back to his corner smarting from those blows to the nose, and Val would always calmly tell him it was okay, "go back in there, you'll figure out how to avoid them." Soon enough, Marvis did, eventually learning to give Willie "payback." It was this kind of progress that told Sam, George, and Val that they had someone special

Chapter 3   Before Larry Holmes : The Amateur Whiz Kid   49

in Marvis Frazier.

Finally, after seven months of boxing workouts and five months of sparring, the staff at Joe Frazier's Gym decided that Marvis was ready for his first fight. Marvis was more than anxious to compete. His dad had recently suggested that he stop his involvement in high school sports to focus on boxing, and Marvis had reluctantly taken Joe's suggestion. So if boxing was going to be his only outlet for the competitive side of his nature, then he wanted to get it on! Not long after, Joe Frazier's team was scheduled to meet the Floyd Patterson Team, and Marvis was given a slot in the lineup. When the big night arrived, Marvis, who was confident in his ability, found himself nervous - almost scared. This was a feeling he would have before every fight for the rest of his career. Fortunately, a few punches into a fight and the feeling would be gone. Unfortunately for the Floyd Patterson boxer, Marvis only needed a few punches to establish his dominance in the match. Marvis easily won by knockout. After the match, Floyd Patterson, a former heavyweight champion himself, was amazed and hit Sam Hickman with, "I thought you said this was young Frazier's first fight?!" "That's right," Sam slyly replied.

Over the next four years, the Marvis Frazier amateur heavyweight train was nearly unstoppable. Sam Hickman would choose the fights and tournaments, George Benton and Val Colbert would do the training, and Marvis Frazier would win. Ten wins and no losses. Twenty wins and no losses. Thirty wins and no losses. Fourty wins and still no losses. During this stretch Marvis was averaging more than one fight every month and winning them all.

Although every fight was important, some were unusually so, like the night Marvis was scheduled to fight a big, strong heavyweight with a mediocre record. Possibly Marvis was getting a bit cocky with his undefeated streak, but he more or less laughed off his teammate Charlie Singleton's suggestion that he be careful with this opponent. Singleton had fought him before, and he remembered that this fighter started off fast and had a powerful right hand. Wouldn't you know it, when the bell rang to start the fight, the big guy rushed across the ring and caught Marvis off guard with a hard right hand. Marvis knew he was hurt and almost knocked out, but he only remembers thinking, "Help me Jesus!" before his own right hand "somehow" caught the jaw of his opponent. Marvis regained total consciousness and a lot of humility. His opponent couldn't make the ten count.

Another time, Marvis entered the ring proudly wearing a new pair of black suede boxing shorts made for him by his mother, Florence. His mom was even watching the fight as he dominated yet another opponent, this time in style. Suddenly, without warning, the referee stopped the contest, looking directly at Marvis. "But sir," Marvis protested, "I'm not hurt!" "No, son," the ref responded, "but you are going to have to do something about those trunks - they're split wide open!" Within minutes, Sam Hickman had figured out a way to patch everything up, much to the relief of an embarrassed heavyweight boxer and his mother!

Then, there was the time highly ranked Tony Tubbs beat Marvis in a close decision to break his undefeated streak. Marvis thought he was "robbed" and needled his friend, Tony, about it after the fight. Tubbs responded with, "Don't worry about it man, the next time we fight it will be for millions!" referring to the fact that both fighters were raising high professional career expectations.

Chapter 3   Before Larry Holmes : The Amateur Whiz Kid

These stories might be listed on the lighter side of being a boxer. However, late in his amateur career Marvis had an experience that fell on a darker side. One night in early 1980, Smokin' Joe had a nightmare that his family was on an airplane that went down in a fiery crash. When Joe learned that Marvis was scheduled to fly to Europe for a tournament just a few weeks later, he took the dream as a premonition and insisted that Marvis bow out. Though he didn't want to miss the tournament, Marvis honored his dad's wishes and withdrew from the match. Then on March 14, 1980, the very jet that Joe asked Marvis not to fly on crashed in Poland, killing all twenty-two members of the American Boxing team on board. Marvis was deeply saddened by the deaths of his many teammates, but also moved by the role played by Smokin' Joe Frazier in his own son's survival.

As the years passed from 1976 to 1978, Marvis got bigger and stronger, and his boxing got better and better. In 1978, at the age of eighteen, Marvis was still undefeated and won the local, regional, and Pennsylvania state Golden Gloves tournaments for a heavyweight. Marvis wanted to go on to challenge at the national level, but Sam Hickman decided he needed one more year's experience. By this time Sam, George, and Val were convinced that Marvis was a great boxer in the making; someone who would someday contend for the heavyweight title of the world; and they weren't about to rush their handiwork. Timing from this point forward would be crucial. Marvis was only eighteen. There was no hurry to get into professional competition. After all, he was the son of a millionaire. He didn't need the money, and the 1980 Olympics were only two years away.

Not long after Marvis embraced the dream of

becoming a boxer and returning the heavyweight championship to the Frazier family, he expanded that dream to include winning a gold medal in the Olympics. Marvis believed that, like his father before him, he would top off his amateur career by capturing the Olympic Gold Medal in the heavyweight division, then move on to the Pros. Now that Marvis was indeed turning out to be an incredible amateur boxer, the Olympic Gold addition to his dream was absolutely possible. As 1979 approached, Sam, George, and Val began to make plans. The fight schedule for Marvis now included many of the top amateur heavyweights in the country, as well as major tournaments throughout the world. There was just over a year before the 1980 Olympic trials would begin, and they wanted Marvis to be ready.

A sweep of tournament victories started for Marvis when he went all the way to National Golden Gloves Heavyweight Champion in 1979. Next, he was crowned Heavyweight Champion and most outstanding Boxer at the Ohio State Fair National Tournament. Early in 1980, Marvis won the Junior Olympic World Heavyweight Championship and was again named Most Outstanding Boxer. Later in the year Marvis captured the coveted A.A.U. (Amateur Athletic Union – now known as USA Boxing) heavyweight title. This title essentially made Marvis the number one amateur heavyweight in the country, and, indeed, shortly thereafter he was recognized as such.

As the 1980 Olympic trials approached, it was certainly no surprise that Marvis Frazier, touting a fifty-four and one record and a string of major tournament victories, was favored to win the heavyweight slot in the trials and take his place on the United States Olympic Team. Once the

Chapter 3   Before Larry Holmes : The Amateur Whiz Kid

trials were underway, Marvis easily defeated his first two opponents and edged closer to being part of the first father/son team to ever win Olympic Medals in boxing. Swelling with confidence, Marvis entered the semi-final round scheduled to fight a big, strong boxer named James Broad. Undaunted by Broad's size, Marvis met him at center ring, ready to rumble. Only seconds later, Marvis Frazier's corner was shocked to see their boxer sprawled motionless on the canvas. No one knew what had happened. Video tape of the brief encounter between the two boxers showed James Broad throwing the first punch during the exchange - a high overhand right. Marvis scrunched down to avoid the hit and prepared to counter with a right of his own. But Marvis never got off the punch. Broad's right hand hit Marvis in the forehead, his body went limp, and he collapsed to the canvas. Marvis knew it wasn't a hard hit, and he wasn't unconscious, yet he was falling. "I'm going down, I'm going down!" he shouted out. Marvis couldn't move, so he couldn't return to the fight. The referee had no choice but to count Marvis out and end the fight. Within fifteen minutes his movement returned and eventually the source of his paralysis was discovered and repaired by neck surgery, but the Amateur Whiz Kid's dream of Olympic Gold had been dashed ... a sad finish to an otherwise remarkable amateur career.

Thirty years after his amateur career ended, Marvis Frazier felt good about the experience, "My amateur career was great. I really enjoyed the chance it gave me to see the world, to see how other people in other cultures live, which helped me to appreciate all the more where I live. I also loved working with my trainers and sparring partners at the gym and fighting against all those great boxers like, Jimmy Clark, Tony Tubbs, Tim Witherspoon, Mitch Green, "Bonecrusher" Smith, and many others. I was disappointed to lose my shot at an Olympic Gold Medal on a fluke injury, but I and my trainers felt I was ready to go professional, ready to move on to the next step in my dream to bring the heavyweight championship back to the Frazier family

(Photo Courtesy of Darryl Lee)

Chapter 4

Before Larry Holmes: The Undefeated Professional

"In the blue corner ... fighting out of Philadelphia, Pennsylvania ... the undefeated Marvis Frazier!"
(Las Vegas ring announcer Chuck Hull)

After his disturbing loss in the Olympic Trials, Marvis Frazier took a vacation. This was quite contrary to his nature. Since deciding he was going to become a boxer and win the heavyweight championship, Marvis had worked almost unceasingly on his dream. But after his disappointing loss to James Broad in the trials, Joe Frazier felt his son needed a break and suggested Marvis take a month off from boxing. Marvis, determined to move forward with his career, was hesitant but, as usual, took his father's advice.

During that month Marvis was a good man to have around the house. It was early summer, and Marvis found the beautiful weather perfect for outside work at the family home. Marvis had always been a big help to his mom by taking care of the yard work, and now he found this same work helping him. It took his mind off boxing and let him relax and enjoy the outdoors. This was reminiscent for Marvis of happy times he had as a boy. Marvis always loved the family trips to Beaufort County, South Carolina, to visit relatives and work on the family plantation, a farm and mansion that his pop had bought after he hit the big time. Marvis enjoyed those trips so much that he actually considered returning there to become a farmer much later in his life. Another thing that helped take his mind off the ring during this vacation from boxing was spending time with his girlfriend, Daralyn Lucas. Marvis and Daralyn had been sweethearts for more than three years and with Marvis taking a break from boxing, this was some of the most uninterrupted free time they had had since they met.

Of course, the time off also gave Marvis time to think, and he just could not help thinking about boxing. While mowing the lawn, pruning the shrubs, or cleaning the pool, Marvis found himself wondering what had happened in that fight against James Broad. How could a fighter with a fifty-six and one record lose so quickly in such an important fight? How could a single weak punch knock him out, when he had never even been knocked down before? Marvis thought about the strange sensation he felt in that fight, going down and while he lay on the canvas. He was conscious yet unable to move. Yes ... there were other times in his life he had experienced the same feeling. There was a time in Junior High School football when he lay on the field stunned after incorrectly tackling a big running back head first. Then, there was a moment in a boxing match with Big Mitch Green that his entire left side went numb after a powerful punch from Big Mitch. Marvis realized that these feelings were the same but had lasted only for seconds, not several minutes as was the case in his loss to James Broad. Something wasn't right about it all, and though he couldn't put his finger on it, Marvis certainly was not about to let it stop him from going forward with his dream. Marvis felt that God had guided him through an exceptional amateur career and had prepared him to take the next step into the professional ranks. Once his vacation was over, that is just what Marvis did.

Chapter 4 Before Larry Holmes : The Undefeated Professional

   While Marvis was taking a break from boxing, his father, Joe, and the staff from the gym were busy making plans for the young man's move up into the professional ranks. First, Joe made sure that everything was still a go. He waited until Marvis had a couple of weeks away from the gym, then asked him if he still wanted to continue boxing. Maybe his son was ready to make a change. Maybe Marvis would be happy to end his career now and leave with the legacy of being one of boxing's great amateur heavyweights. Joe did not presume one way or the other and did not pressure Marvis in his decision, though he certainly was happy when his son stated that he absolutely wanted to become a professional boxer. Following this response, Joe got together with George Benton and Val Colbert to make specific plans. Sam Hickman would not be a member of the management team directing Marvis's professional career. He had an important job as the scout for the amateur fighters in Joe Frazier's Gym and could not easily perform that job and scout for Marvis's professional fights as well. Smokin' Joe would take over that role for Marvis, although as his friend, Sam would continue to give Marvis career advice whenever he sought it. While George Benton and Val Colbert would continue as Marvis's trainers, Joe would join them in the corner as well, adding a source of great pride for Marvis to have his pop in his corner. Though this also put some added pressure on his performance, not just to win but to win in a way his pop would be proud of.
   A bit later in the summer of 1980, after Marvis had returned to his daily routine at the gym, Joe began negotiations with the people at Madison Square Garden in New York. Madison Square Garden was one of the busiest sports arenas in the world and the site of many of Joe's

own fights, including "The Fight of the Century" with Muhammad Ali in 1971, the fight that gave Joe universal recognition as the heavyweight champion of the world after he soundly defeated Ali. It was only smart business to consider that the son of Smokin' Joe might also be a big draw as he tried to follow in the footsteps of his famous father, especially after such an illustrious amateur career of his own. Joe used this incentive to negotiate a deal. Marvis would get an opportunity to stage his first several professional bouts at the prestigious Madison Square Garden, and the Garden management would take a chance that Marvis could continue his amateur winning ways as a professional.

In those days, the major boxing events were held in the main Madison Square Garden Arena, which seated nearly twenty-thousand people. Lesser known boxing events with up and coming boxers took place in the Theater at Madison Square Garden. This area held up to five thousand spectators and was known as the Felt Forum. Joe Frazier worked out a deal for Marvis that included three fights in the Felt Forum, followed by a fourth fight in the Arena. The opponents for Marvis were suggested by the Madison Square Garden Matchmaker and okayed by Smokin' Joe.

The first professional opponent selected for Marvis Frazier was a young, tall, beginning boxer who had been a wide receiver in the former World Football League. It was scheduled to take place in the Felt Forum at Madison Square Garden. The date chosen was September 12th, 1980, Marvis's twentieth birthday.

Professional Fight Number One
Date: September 12, 1980
Place: Felt Forum at Madison Square Garden, New York, New York
Opponent: Roger Troupe

This turned out to be a big fight for Marvis in many ways. It was his first professional fight and ended up being his first professional win. It was his twentieth birthday, five years after he had committed himself to his dream of becoming a professional boxer. It was the first fight for Marvis after his mysterious loss to James Broad in the Olympic trials and it was the first time his father, Smokin' Joe, would be in his corner.

Marvis Frazier's opponent that night in the Felt Forum was Roger Troupe. Troupe was fighting out of Vineland, New Jersey. He had been boxing professionally for about two years and had a modest three and four record, but Troupe was known more for his stint as a wide receiver for the Philadelphia Bell of the World Football League. He was built like a wide receiver at 6' 2'' and 207 lbs.

Before the fight started that night, Marvis's birthday was announced, and the crowd sang *Happy Birthday* to him. Then it was announced that Smokin' Joe Frazier was present, and Joe took a bow while the crowd applauded. During this time, Marvis felt that nervous, almost scared, feeling that he got before every fight. Marvis was absolutely confident that he would win, since he had trained hard and Val Colbert had helped him work out the "key" to a victory, but this nervous feeling had become routine.

Normally after a few punches were thrown the feeling would pass, but well into the first round of this fight Marvis was looking tense, not yet smooth, in his maneuvering around the ring. The Madison Square Garden announcer,

John Condon, mentioned that Marvis was suffering from "Gardenitis" not long before Marvis seemed to settle down to some serious boxing. Neither fighter was hesitant to throw punches as they mixed it up from the start, though not many punches were landing effectively. Finally, with less than a minute left in the first round, Marvis seemed to get his rhythm going. He danced around Troupe and scored heavily with combinations of punches. Undaunted, Roger Troupe came right back. With ten seconds left in the round, Troupe hit Frazier hard with a right and followed with another right and a hard left. Marvis was definitely hurt, and had he not ducked another big right while he lay on the ropes just before the round ended, Troupe may well have had the win. The hits from Troupe were all solid, but Marvis believes the neck injury magnified the damage. He felt the tingling sensation in his extremities after Troupe's first hard right, and as Marvis walked back to his corner at the end of that first round, he stumbled a bit, like someone suffering from partial paralysis might.

Whether or not the neck injury had magnified the damage from Troupe's barrage at the end of the first round, seeing his son almost knocked out in the first round of his first professional fight affected Smokin' Joe. Joe kept his composure in the corner, but he was angry with his son's shaky start. Meanwhile, Marvis started taking control of the fight in the second round. Roger Troupe never backed down. Instead, multiple combinations from Marvis wore him down. About one minute into the second round, a long overhand right by Marvis knocked Troupe right out of the ring. It looked very impressive, but Troupe somehow managed to get back in the ring and made it through the round. In the third round, Roger Troupe showed a lot of guts and determination, but an endless barrage of scoring punches from Marvis was quickly taking its toll. With about one minute left in the round, Marvis pinned Troupe on the ropes and hit him with one combination of punches after another. Finally, Roger Troupe went down in a heap and the fight was stopped.

After a close call, Marvis Frazier had won his first professional fight by knockout! Marvis, who didn't normally gloat after a win, was so happy that he was jumping for joy around the ring. What a great birthday present! Joe Frazier, on the other hand, was happy for the win but anguished about the fight. In the post fight interview with John Condon, Joe said, "I don't know if I can take too much of this. There are going to have to be some changes. I will make changes." And, indeed, he did. By the next fight, Joe Frazier was the head trainer for his son. The great George Benton had been demoted.

Record: One Win   No Losses   One Knockout
Professional Fight Number Two
Date: October 10, 1980
Place: Felt Forum at Madison Square Garden, New York, New York
Opponent: Dennis Rivers

Marvis's second professional fight was again in the Felt Forum at Madison Square Garden in New York City. His opponent was another tall, young boxer fighting out of New Jersey. Dennis Rivers stood at 6' 3" and weighed 210 pounds. For Marvis, the trainer card deck had been reshuffled – his father was the head trainer while George Benton and Val Colbert were now co-assistant trainers. Both fighters had one win and no losses.

In the first round, the two fighters seemed to be just feeling each other out. Rivers was using his height and weight advantage to push Marvis around the ring, though Marvis pushed right back. There were a minimum of punches thrown in the first round and even less were successfully landed. It was an even match at the end of three minutes. In the second round, Marvis Frazier picked up the pace. Now Marvis was doing the pushing, but he was doing it with punches. Marvis bearing in and Dennis Rivers backing up. Marvis punching, punching, punching driving Rivers back. About half way through the round, Rivers looked like he was in trouble, but he was hanging on. Then, with just under a minute left, Marvis unleashed literally dozens of punches of every type and from every direction. With thirty seconds remaining in the second round, referee Joe Cortez stopped the fight just as Rivers dropped to his hands and knees on the canvas. Both fighters started the night undefeated, but by the second round it was obvious that Dennis Rivers was no match for Marvis Frazier.

Record: Two Wins   No Losses   Two knockouts
Professional Fight Number Three
Date: April 10, 1981
Place: Felt Forum at Madison Square Garden, New York, New York
Opponent: Melvin Epps

After two quick wins in two months, Marvis would have to wait six months for his third contest, but for good reason. The neck injury that had resulted in his loss to James Broad in the Olympic trials showed itself again during practice in November. Just one month after he defeated Dennis Rivers, Marvis was stricken with paralysis while sparring at his dad's gym with Jimmy Young. This time there was no mistaking the injury for a knockout.

Marvis was fully conscious but unable to move. When his sensation and movement finally came back after nearly a quarter of an hour, Marvis was taken to Dr. Joseph Fabiani, an orthopedist who had worked with the Frazier camp for years. Dr. Fabiani performed some tests by physical manipulation (these were the days before MRI's, etc.) and sent Marvis to Dr. Frederick Simeone, a neurosurgeon. An operation to reduce the risk of a re-occurrence of the paralysis was performed by Dr. Simeone shortly thereafter.

So, although his third professional fight was against a boxer whose record was only five wins and four losses, the stakes were significantly higher because it was a fight to test his post operative physical condition. Marvis had no fear of causing complications by continuing his career. He trusted that God was in control of his life, and Dr. Simeone had assured him that it was safe to return to the ring.

His opponent for fight number three was Melvin Epps. Melvin was the smallest heavyweight that Marvis would face in his professional career. Epps weighed only 184 pounds and was not an aggressive fighter. Yet Melvin Epps would have a full professional heavyweight career spanning some thirteen years. Over those dozen odd years, Epps would face the likes of Mitch Green, Philipp Brown, Renaldo Snipes, and Lennox Lewis. For his fight with Marvis on April 10th of 1981, Epps kept a defensive posture throughout the match and stayed on the run. Marvis chased Epps around the ring for all six rounds. The neck injury was never really put to the test but the victory was never in doubt. No knockout this time, but the decision was unanimous.

Record: Three Wins No Losses Two Knockouts
Professional Fight Number Four
Date: May 11, 1981
Place: The Arena in Madison Square Garden, New York, New York
Opponent: Steve Zouski

    Finally, after three fights in the Felt Forum, Marvis had his shot at The Arena in Madison Square Garden. His fight against veteran heavyweight Steve Zouski was the under card for the main event featuring up and coming Gerry Cooney versus the old war horse Ken Norton. As a preliminary fight to the nationally televised main event, the match between Marvis and Steve Zouski was taped and replayed to the national audience while the main event contenders were preparing for their fight. The announcers for the Cooney/Norton main event, Larry Merchant and Sugar Ray Leonard, also covered the Marvis Frazier/Steve Zouski fight and heaped praise on Marvis. "Marvis's punches are short and fast." "Marvis is rather impressive." "Marvis looks very composed." "Marvis is much more of a boxer than his father Joe." The two announcers gushed about Marvis, while pointing out that Zouski was the toughest and most experienced opponent for Marvis to date. Marvis took control of the fight from the opening bell, controlled the tempo throughout, and looked far more experienced than a twenty year old with only three previous professional bouts under his belt.
    Steve Zouski, listed in the Who's Who of Polish Americans, was twenty-seven years old and had already fought twenty-two times when he and Marvis squared off at the Garden. His twenty-one and one record with fourteen knockouts made him by far the best boxer Marvis had faced in his eight months as a professional. Zouski

Chapter 4   Before Larry Holmes : The Undefeated Professional

would go on to scrap his way through a fourteen year professional career including fights against Mike Tyson, George Foreman, Tommy Morrison, Tony Tubbs, and Jose Ribalta. In his career overall, Steve won more than he lost. But on this night, on national television, against a young Marvis Frazier, he was out punched at a five to one ratio, and the best he could hope for was to make it to the end of the fight standing. Even this was denied him though, when in the sixth and final round referee Billy Graham (not that Billy Graham!) watched Zouski absorb eleven, consecutive, unanswered, scoring punches from Frazier and stopped the fight.

Less than one month after his convincing win over Steve Zouski was broadcast to a national audience, Marvis Frazier was pictured with his dad on the cover of Sports Illustrated. "The Chip Off the Old Champ" was starting to get noticed.

Record: Four Wins No Losses Three Knockouts
Professional Fight Number Five
Date: August 22, 1981
Place: Showboat Casino, Las Vegas, Nevada
Opponent: Tony Pulu

After three fights in the Felt Forum and one in the Arena, Joe Frazier's dealings with Madison Square Garden were done. Marvis then went on what could have been called the Casino Circuit, staging five of his next six fights at casinos in Las Vegas and Atlantic City. The first of these five was at the Showboat Hotel and Casino in Las Vegas against a Polynesian boxer named Tony Pulu. Pulu had been boxing professionally since the early 1970's when he had won a lot of fights against unknown boxers, but he had been on a losing streak in the year and a half leading up to his match with Marvis. For Marvis, Pulu provided a good learning opportunity at this point in his career, because Tony Pulu was a big, hard hitter with a very awkward style. The way he stood, the positioning of his hands, and how he threw his punches all presented Marvis with challenges he had not faced before. Marvis, however, was easily up for the task. Having sparred with so many different boxers in his dad's gym as a regular part of his workout routine, Marvis was not taken by surprise with anything Pulu had to offer. After the very first exchange of the fight, Marvis adjusted to Pulu's style, stunned the big Polynesian with a short right hand, then dominated his opponent for the remainder of the fight. To tough Tony Pulu's credit, he managed to go the distance despite a rain of blows from Frazier for all six rounds. It was a unanimous decision but not a knockout.

Record: Five Wins No Losses Three Knockouts
Professional Fight Number Six
Date: September 16, 1981
Place: Caesar's Palace, Las Vegas, Nevada
Opponent: Guy Casale

Less than a month later and just days before his twenty-first birthday, Marvis took on a guy named Guy. Guy "The Rock" Casale was a boxer out of Newark, New Jersey, who not only looked like Rocky Marciano but fought a lot like him too: get close to your opponent, punch hard to the body, and try for hooks to the head. Obviously Casale didn't succeed to the same degree as the great Marciano, but he did manage to win fourteen of his twenty fights, knockout Bobby Halpern as the main event at Madison

Chapter 4 Before Larry Holmes : The Undefeated Professional   67

Square Garden in 1978, and get elected to the New Jersey Boxing Hall of Fame. At the time of Guy Casale's match with Marvis, he was still undecided as to whether to continue his boxing career. Though Casale had won his previous four fights by knockout, he was still recovering from a shoulder injury that had required two operations. As it turned out, this fight with Marvis Frazier would be his last.

The fight itself took place outside at Caesar's Palace in Las Vegas. It was the under card fight for the first encounter between Sugar Ray Leonard and Thomas Hearns. Casale actually took the fight to Marvis in the first round, as he kept backing Frazier up with hard punches to the body. In the second round, Marvis began a steady left jab to keep Casale back. In the third round, Marvis kept up the jab but added combinations, with shots coming from all directions. Midway through the third round, Marvis was overwhelming Casale. Announcer Marv Albert described the scene as, "Marvis Frazier scoring continuously, putting on a clinic of different punches." The onslaught continued in the fourth and at the end of the round, Marvis put Guy Casale against the ropes with a clean right hand and then followed up with eight straight scoring hits as Casale leaned against the ropes for support. Courageously, Casale survived the round, but after being looked at by Dr. Donald Romeo before the fifth round began, the fight was stopped. Over two decades later, Guy "The Gentleman" Casale would tell a reporter what an honor it was for him to be on the fight card that night and to battle a boxer who went on to fight Larry Holmes for the world title.

Record: Six Wins No Losses Four Knockouts
Professional Fight Number Seven
Date: February 8, 1983
Place: Tropicana Hotel & Casino, Atlantic City, New Jersey

Opponent: Amos Haynes

The Frazier management team liked to keep Marvis busy with lots of fights. While he was an amateur, Marvis averaged slightly more than one fight per month. Except for the time required for recuperation from neck surgery after his second pro fight, Marvis was setting a similar pace as a young professional. Now, that pace was going to be altered again.

Sickness was going to keep Marvis out of the ring for nearly a year and a half. First, there was a simple ear infection which showed up in October 1981, about a month after Marvis's win over Guy Casale. The ear infection seemed like a minor problem for Marvis, so initially he did not seek medical attention, hoping it would simply pass. However, after a couple of weeks, the ear became quite painful and Marvis had a fever. While in the ring for his usual sparring shift, Marvis had started to experience dizziness. The ear infection had obviously intensified and medical care was necessary. Ear infections in adults can be either bacterial or viral. An ear infection caused by bacteria is easier to treat than one that is viral, so it is prudent to assume a bacterial cause and use antibiotics for treatment. If handling the infection with antibiotics is successful, then the determination of the cause and the cure are both accomplished in a single step. If the antibiotics do not succeed, then the cause is shown to be viral and an alternative treatment must be utilized. Unfortunately, the use of antibiotics was unsuccessful for Marvis and treatment for a viral source of his ear infection had to be initiated. Finally, after Marvis was out of commission for nearly two months, the infection was gone from his ear. Yet even then he was still physically run down from the

Chapter 4 Before Larry Holmes: The Undefeated Professional

experience and would have to build himself back up.

With the ear infection gone, Marvis was confident he could finally return to his routine in the gym and get himself back into fighting shape. So once he had the okay, Marvis returned with a vengeance, determined to make up for lost time. At first everything seemed fine, but within a couple of weeks of his return to the gym, Marvis wasn't feeling right again. He thought the ear infection might have come back, but the symptoms weren't really the same. Instead of dizziness Marvis was experiencing tiredness and lack of energy. Having only recently returned to training, Marvis was in no mood for another interruption, so he continued to work out despite his feeling less like doing so each day. Finally, when a low grade fever and loss of appetite were added to the original symptoms of tiredness and lack of energy, Marvis decided to seek medical advice. To his surprise, Marvis was diagnosed with hepatitis. His symptoms (which eventually included jaundice) plus some simple tests performed by the doctor indicated inflammation of the liver. Although Marvis was in a gym on a daily basis at a time when passing food from one person to another and sharing water from a common bucket was customary, he never knew for sure how he contracted the disease. His symptoms were mild over all and had no long term effects, but they were severe enough to keep him out of boxing for over a year, just at a time when he was working his way toward becoming a contender.

Between the ear infection and hepatitis, Marvis had to endure a long period of inactivity before he could climb back into the ring. Finally though, after a seventeen month delay, Marvis did climb back into the ring.

The ring was in Atlantic City, the date was February

8th, 1983, and his opponent was Amos Haynes. Amos Haynes was not the best Marvis had faced. Haynes had a losing record in a fairly short career and had lost five straight prior to fighting Marvis. Joe had intentionally selected a weaker fighter to help Marvis ease back into the feel of competition after such a long layoff. The fight was scheduled for ten rounds, and it took Marvis a few rounds to get the cobwebs out, but by the fifth round, Marvis had Haynes down twice and referee Joe O'Neil stopped the contest. Even more important was how well Marvis had held up physically. His battles with sickness where definitely behind him.

Record: Seven Wins No Losses Five Knockouts
Professional Fight Number Eight
Date: March 7, 1983
Place: Charleston, South Carolina
Opponent: Mike Cohen

With a clean bill of health and another win under his belt, Marvis was flying high going into his next fight. Marvis felt like God was with him, and he could feel the spirit of God in him. This was powerful motivation for Marvis to keep on doing what he was doing. Poor Mike Cohen, his next opponent, having to fight a talented, healthy, and motivated Marvis Frazier. On top of all that, the fight was being held in South Carolina where Marvis was born and a lot of his extended family still lived. Of course, all those aunts, uncles, and cousins from both sides of the family were there to cheer "Marvie" on. "Oooh, Marvie, look at young Marvie, you're doin' good, Marvie!"

Mike Cohen was really a pretty good boxer. He, too, was from South Carolina and boasted a fourteen and three record coming into his contest with "young Marvie." However, Cohen hit a buzzsaw that night - an assassin. Marvis went right to work in the first round and finished him off in the second.

Oooh, Marvie - you did good, Marvie!

Record: Eight Wins No Losses Six Knockouts
Professional Fight Number Nine
Date: April 10, 1983
Place: Resorts International, Atlantic City, New Jersey
Opponent: James Broad

In a way, this was the fight Marvis had been waiting for since he turned professional on his birthday in September of 1980. Of course, his dream was to win the heavyweight crown, but after losing his final fight as an amateur and a shot at an Olympic Gold Medal, Marvis always hoped for a re-match with James Broad. This fight was a chance to make up for that loss or "get his name back" as his pop would repeat over and over in the workouts leading up to the contest.

James Broad was the fighter who threw the fluke punch that had put Marvis down (but not out) in the Olympic trials in the early summer of 1980. At the time, Broad was a relative unknown, while Marvis was favored to make the Olympic team. In the three years since, James "Broad Axe" Broad had also turned professional and had made a big splash with twelve victories in a row, including seven knockouts. The WBC (World Boxing Council) had him ranked as the number fourteen heavyweight fighter in the world. A fight with Broad would not only give Marvis a chance to "get his name back" and show that the Olympic trials loss was indeed a fluke, but it would give him an opportunity to battle against a bona fide ranked heavyweight.

The opportunity to battle Broad could not have come at a better time. After his eight consecutive wins as a professional, Marvis was full of confidence in his abilities as a boxer and overflowing with enthusiasm about his career. He looked at a fight with Broad as the next logical step up the stairway leading to the heavyweight championship. Since James Broad was moving in a similar direction, this fight had the makings of a great one.

And a great fight it was! Two game heavyweights who were young, undefeated, and both looking toward the title. It was the main event on CBS Sports Sunday. The commentators were Sugar Ray Leonard, Gil Clancy, and Tim Ryan. The stands were filled with fans for both fighters.

The first round started out slowly with both boxers dancing around looking for openings. Very few punches were thrown. In round two the fighters started to mix it up. James Broad swung that "Broad Axe" by throwing some big punches. About half way through the round, just as Sugar Ray Leonard was imploring Frazier to move inside on Broad, Marvis stepped inside Broad's big swings and started punching. A sweeping right hand counter punch by Marvis caught Broad flush on the chin, and seemingly from out of nowhere the big guy was in trouble. Marvis followed with another right hand that put Broad against the ropes, dazed. Marvis went over and under with a flurry of punches to try to finish him off, but Broad stayed alive to take the fight to the next round.

For the next couple of rounds, Marvis controlled the action and even dropped his gloves a few times to taunt Broad. During those rounds, numerous short punches by

Frazier opened a cut above Broad's left eye. Gil Clancy declared it a, "Marvelous performance by Marvis Frazier, just marvelous." In the middle rounds, the pace slowed but neither fighter backed down from the other. Many blows were exchanged and the endurance of both men was put to the test. With one minute left in the seventh round, Broad laid a big hit on Marvis as they went into the ropes, but he was too tired to keep up an effective attack and let Marvis escape. The fighters were evenly matched in the eighth round, but Marvis came roaring out in the ninth, moving from side to side to punish Broad with a variety of punches from all directions. James Broad's legs wobbled, but the ninth round came to an end before Marvis could put him down.

In the final round, a weary James Broad felt he needed a knockout to win and rushed out swinging. Marvis didn't back down, and it was a wild fight to the finish with both boxers scoring heavily. Before it was over, the commentators expressed their admiration for the two. Gil Clancy belted out, "What a heavyweight fight!" Tim Ryan replied, "These two young men have really put on a show!" It was the kind of boxing that inspires people to love the sport. And when it was all over, the two combatants affectionately embraced, smiling and showing their mutual respect. It was close, but the winner, by unanimous decision and still undefeated was Marvis Frazier!

Record: Nine Wins No Losses Six Knockouts
Professional Fight Number Ten
Date: June 4, 1983
Place: Sands Casino Hotel, Atlantic City, New Jersey
Opponent: Joe Bugner

Joe Bugner was a world class heavyweight boxer. He may have been the best European heavyweight ever. His career spanned four decades during which he fought eighty-three times, winning sixty-nine and capturing numerous titles. In the 1970's Bugner was ranked among the top five heavyweight contenders in the world. During his career Joe Bugner fought: Henry Cooper, Jimmy Ellis, Muhammad Ali (twice), Ron Lyle, Earnie Shavers, James Tillis, and Smokin' Joe Frazier. Joe Bugner also fought Marvis Frazier.

In 1983, at the age of thirty-three, after winning his previous four fights by knockout while working on a career comeback, world class heavyweight boxer Joe Bugner agreed to fight the son of the great boxer he had battled ten years earlier. Although he lost the decision to Smokin' Joe Frazier in 1973, many consider that classic bout to be Bugner's best career performance. Defeating Marvis Frazier would keep his comeback streak alive and could give him some sense of payback for the loss to Joe ten years prior.

For Marvis, it was his first shot at a world class heavyweight and a chance to equal or surpass something done by his dad. In 1980, Marvis had failed to qualify for the Olympic boxing team and therefore fell short of one his dad's accomplishments. But now, with this fight he could beat a boxer his dad had beaten, and if he could knock Joe Bugner out, he would surpass what his dad had done in his fight with Joe Bugner. Of course, Joe Bugner, who was as tough as nails, had only been knocked out twice in his career.

The fight between Joe Bugner and Marvis Frazier took place seven weeks after Marvis's fight with James Broad, and like that fight was the main event on CBS sports. Gil Clancy, who was fast becoming a Marvis Frazier fan, was again one of the CBS commentators. Clancy and his co-commentator, Tim Ryan,

Chapter 4 Before Larry Holmes : The Undefeated Professional

repeatedly complimented Marvis for his speed, conditioning, intensity, volume of punches, and enthusiasm. Gil Clancy even went so far as to mention that in the amateurs Marvis had outranked many of the boxers now being considered for title fights against the heavyweight champion, Larry Holmes. Then, Clancy unintentionally provided the viewers with foreshadowing when he speculated that Marvis Frazier may have a title shot sooner that anyone realizes – this, only six months before Marvis Frazier did, indeed, get a shot to fight Larry Holmes for the title!

As for the fight, it really looked liked the boxing version of David versus Goliath. Marvis never took the giant out, but he chased him all over the ring and relentlessly pounded him with punches from start to finish. In the end, there was a unanimous decision for Marvis Frazier and a sporting hug between the contestants. In Marvis's mind, everything was going according to plan.

Record: Ten Wins No Losses Six knockouts

Several weeks after Marvis defeated Joe Bugner on June 4th, 1983, he married his high school sweetheart, Daralyn Evon Lucas. Twenty-eight years later, Marvis recalled the following incident that occurred while he and his bride were enjoying their honeymoon on a cruise ship somewhere in the Caribbean.

"One of the stewards on the ship came to our dining table to tell me that I had a phone call. Thinking it might be an emergency at home, I excused myself from my dinner date with Daralyn and went to take the call. When I got to the phone, it was Pop.

'Hey son, you wanna fight Larry Holmes?'

'What are you talking about? I'm on my honeymoon!

What are you doing calling me here?!'

'Do - you - want - to - fight - Larry - Holmes - for - the - championship?'

'We'll talk about it later. I don't want to talk about it now. I'm on my honeymoon.'

'C'mon man, you wanna fight him or not?'

'Look Pop, you know I'll fight anybody.'

" When I got back to the table I told Daralyn about the call.

She looked at me and replied, 'That's a wonderful opportunity, Marvis... but do you really think you're ready for Larry Holmes?"

Years later Marvis and Daralyn enjoy a dinner together, without interruption. (Photo Courtesy of Webster Riddick)

Chapter 5

After Larry Holmes: Two Strikes, But Not Out

In response to Larry Holmes's statement that he would fight at least four more fights in order to have a shot at Rocky Marciano's record, Marvis Frazier told a reporter at Jet Magazine, "I hope, I wish, I pray that he does ... and that I be the forty-ninth (opponent)."

Two months before his fight with Larry Holmes, "lookout" man for Joe Frazier's Gym, Sam Hickman told Marvis Frazier that he was not yet ready to face the champion. Sam, who had helped pick the opponents for Marvis throughout his amateur career, didn't doubt his potential to become the heavyweight champion but felt that Marvis needed more ring time against experienced fighters like Joe Bugner before challenging for the championship. Joe Frazier, as his son's trainer and manager, felt that the cards had fallen into place for his son's shot at the title and wanted to take advantage of the opportunity. Marvis was flying high after beating Bugner in June of 1983, for his tenth consecutive professional win and was so full of youthful confidence and a sense of purpose in his pursuit of the heavyweight championship of the world that he believed he could beat anyone, even the unbeaten Larry Holmes.

And yet, when Larry's booming overhand right sent Marvis sprawling to the canvas at two minutes and six seconds into the first round of their November, 1983, contest, the first thought that came to mind for young Marvis as he lay face down was, "maybe Sam Hickman was right, maybe I'm not ready for Larry Holmes." When the fight was stopped by referee Mills Lane less than a minute later, Marvis's momentary doubt turned to utter dispair, and the question of whether he had taken on Holmes too soon would linger in his soul for years to come.

In the meantime, a devastated Marvis Frazier went politely and responsibly through the post fight routine that night at Caesar's Palace, including a twenty-some minute press conference, though what he really wanted to do was find the proverbial hole to crawl into and hide from the reality of how much he felt he had "messed up." Finally, when the reporters had run out of questions, Marvis escaped to his hotel room and the solace of his wife Daralyn. The very next morning, Marvis and Daralyn left Las Vegas by plane for California. They were accompanied by Mark, one of Marvis's cousins on his father's side, who was a fellow boxer and member of the entourage that led Marvis into the ring before the fight. Marvis loved all of his cousins on both sides of the family, but he and Mark were nearly the same age and easily shared their feelings with each other. Marvis was being consoled by his wife Daralyn but since he was emotionally in a state of shock, maybe Mark could help. The quick trip to California was not a preplanned vacation but an attempt to separate Marvis physically from Nevada. Once in California, the three engulfed themselves in entertainment activities meant to take Marvis's mind off the fight, including comedy clubs and Disneyland. At one of the comedy clubs, performer Keenan Wayans spotted Marvis and took the opportunity to kid with him, pointing Marvis out to the audience and making the joke that his watch had stopped at 2:57 - the time that had passed in the

Chapter 5   After Larry Holmes : Two Strikes, But Not Out   79

first round against Holmes before referee Mills Lane had stopped the fight. Marvis laughed, but somewhere deep inside him, a clock had indeed stopped when Mills Lane halted the contest. In his mind, it was as though all of his hopes and dreams had come crashing down, and Marvis did not even want to look at the wreckage. The first night in California, Marvis, though he did not drink, bought two bottles of champagne, consumed their entire contents, and promptly passed out until morning.

After about a week in California, the trio returned home to Philadelphia. Throughout his boxing career, Marvis would return to his workout routine in his dad's gym immediately after a fight, many times the very next day. Not so now. Though a week had passed since his loss to Larry Holmes, Marvis still could not face returning to the gym. Joe Frazier was aware of his son's state of mind and thoughtfully suggested he take some time off. Marvis gladly consented. He spent most of his down time with Daralyn, looking for a new house. Since their marriage in July of 1983, the young couple had been living at Daralyn's childhood home, but now that Daralyn was pregnant with their first child, they wanted to set up a home in their own house.

As the days became weeks and the weeks became months, that Marvis did not show up at the gym and had no new fights scheduled, rumors began to circulate that Marvis Frazier was done, that he was retiring from boxing. However, there was no truth to these rumors. During his time off after the loss to Holmes, Marvis Frazier was not considering retiring from his chosen profession or abandoning his dream to return the heavyweight championship to the Frazier family. Instead, Marvis was using the break from boxing to try to "get his head right." He was trying to clear out a feeling of failure and re-focus his thoughts on a new strategy. Eight months after his loss to Larry Holmes, just before his twenty-fourth birthday, Marvis was ready to begin again.

The new strategy for Marvis after his loss to Larry Holmes was simple, use his very respectable ten and one record to lure top ranked contenders into the ring, and beat anyone unfortunate enough to take the bait. The theory was that, after enough wins against top contenders, the Holmes management would accept the idea that the loss by Marvis to their man was mostly a matter of inexperience and that now Frazier had the experience to deserve a rematch. Of course, with numerous wins against ranked contenders, Marvis would be highly ranked himself and would have some clout if the Holmes people tried to avoid giving him another shot. Holmes gave credibility to this strategy when, within months after beating Marvis he announced that he would not retire until he had fought enough fights to have a chance to break Rocky Marciano's lifetime undefeated record of forty-nine wins and no losses.

Another strategy that Marvis and his father could have pursued to get Marvis a heavyweight title would have been for them to seek a title fight with the boxer crowned as "world champion" by one of the other professional boxing governing bodies. For example, the WBA (World Boxing Association) had a revolving door-like series of four different champions from 1983 through 1986. All four were fighters that Marvis could likely have beaten, but Marvis wanted to beat the best and that was clearly Larry Holmes. Holmes was the true linear champion of the great heavyweight champions that extended back to Muhammed Ali, and Marvis's father Smokin' Joe. Larry Holmes was definitely the man Marvis wanted to beat to win his heavyweight title -- unless, of course, someone

Chapter 5   After Larry Holmes : Two Strikes, But Not Out

else beat Larry first ...

So, by May of 1984, Marvis was back in his dad's gym working on the comeback trail that would return him to the ring in a rematch with Holmes. His gym routine was the same: morning road work, back at the gym for loosening up and jumping rope, shadow boxing, working the heavy bag, speed bag, reflex bag, medicine ball and/or hand pads, and of course sparring - lots of sparring. Once a boxer is in shape, sparring is by far the best means to practice and improve skills. Training at Joe Frazier's Gym gave Marvis incredible sparring opportunities because there were so many great fighters in attendance. One of the reasons Marvis could defend himself so well against various boxing styles was that he sparred against so many different boxers at his dad's gym.

Over the years, Marvis sparred against dozens of talented boxers, including:

Marvin Stinson (who was once called boxing's #1 sparring partner) "I learned a lot from Marvin Stinson. He was a great teacher and a great, great boxer." - Marvis

Pinklon Thomas (WBC Heavyweight Champ from August, 1984, until March, 1986) "Pinklon was a great fighter. He and I had some real battles when we sparred." - Marvis

Randall Tex Cobb (Tough, tough fighter who went toe to toe with the likes of Earnie Shavers, Ken Norton, and Larry Holmes as a professional boxer before becoming a successful Hollywood actor in such movies as *Raising Arizona* and *Uncommon Valor*) "Randall Tex Cobb was a good puncher and could take a lot of punches. It was like boxing a bag of cement when I sparred with Randall." - Marvis

Tim Witherspoon (An excellent boxer who was crowned heavyweight champion by four different governing bodies over an eight year period from the mid 1980's through the early 1990's) "Tim Witherspoon was a good, good guy. He helped me a lot as an experienced sparring partner, when I was preparing for the Holmes fight." - Marvis

Dwight Triplett (Once fought Carl "The Truth" Williams) "Dwight Tripplet was more or less a sparring partner by profession. He worked hard as a sparring partner, and he knew how to make me work hard." - Marvis

Jimmy Young (Another skillful Philadelphia boxer, active during the 1970's and early 1980's when he fought Ken Norton, Earnie Shavers, Ron Lyle, Gerry Cooney, Muhammad Ali - for the title in a close loss, and George Foreman – who he defeated) "The hardest guy in the world to hit. He was able to get away almost every time." - Marvis

Rodney Frazier (First cousin to Marvis, Rodney had a professional career as a heavyweight, ending up with sixteen wins out of twenty fights) "We sparred a lot. Sometimes he would get me, and sometimes I would get him." - Marvis

Willie "the Worm" Monroe (A great middleweight fighter who defeated Marvin Hagler in the 1970's, Monroe was one of the first professional fighters Marvis sparred against as a young amateur) "Willie taught me how to slip jabs, because that guy would pound my nose and I had to

Chapter 5 After Larry Holmes : Two Strikes, But Not Out

roll and slip just to get out of the way of those punches."
- Marvis

Michael Spinks (One half of the famous Spinks Jinx with his brother Leon, Michael Spinks was an outstanding amateur boxer, who won the 1976 Olympic Gold Medal as a middleweight. Michael was, of course, also a great professional, winning titles as both a light-heavyweight and a heavyweight. His heavyweight belt came at the expense of Larry Holmes, who was denied Rocky Marciano's undefeated lifetime record by Michael's fifteen round unanimous decision win) "I sparred with Michael Spinks a couple of times. They were great fights – we had wars!"
- Marvis

James "Bonecrusher" Smith (A big, strong fighter who turned professional at the late age of twenty-eight and at one point held the WBA title for about four months) "Bonecrusher and I went back a long ways. We sparred, fought twice as amateurs, and eventually fought professionally." - Marvis

Bert Cooper ("Smokin'" Bert Cooper was a product of Joe Frazier's Gym, who went on to challenge for both the cruiserweight and heavyweight crowns in numerous wild and memorable fights) "Tough, tough fighter with great potential. Everyone thought he was a member of our family." - Marvis

Dwight Muhammad Qawi (A short fighter at 5'6" Dwight Muhammad Qawi had more than fifty fights covering a twenty year professional career, during which he held titles in both the cruiserweight and light-heavyweight divisions)

"Dwight would get so frustrated when we sparred, because he had a hard time getting a good piece of me." - Marvis

Marvis even sparred with that fairly famous fighter Smokin' Joe Frazier a couple of times, though he learned less about boxing and more about life in those two encounters.

The first was when Marvis was about thirteen years old. Marvis wasn't even a boxer then and the "sparring session" took place in the basement of the Frazier's home. It seems that Marvis was in a mischievous mood one day at home, after school. His sister, Jacqui, had a way of getting on his nerves just because she was always reading or writing something, and she was up to it again on this particular afternoon. Marvis always tried to bother her when he caught her studying. This time by throwing a pillow at her. He picked up a couch pillow and hit her with it from across the room. "Marvis you'd better stop!" Jacqui warned as she shrugged off the hit and returned to her writing. "What are you going to do about it?" Marvis jested as he reached for a second pillow. "You just better stop," his sister replied firmly. Of course, Marvis let the pillow fly, hitting Jacqui square in the head. That was it. Jacquelyn charged over to Marvis and slapped his face. Marvis reacted with an uppercut to the midsection. Marvis didn't mean to, but he hit her hard. Jacqui ran from the room crying. Jacqui found mom, then mom found Marvis. "What are you doing hitting your sister?" His mom hollered. "Go to your room right now!" followed by the monster words that kids dread, "Wait 'til your father gets home!" Panic rushed through his head - "No! Oh God, No!" he thought to himself and half out loud.

Since it was only 5:30, and the executioner didn't get home until after eleven, Marvis had several hours to

Chapter 5   After Larry Holmes : Two Strikes, But Not Out   85

agonize over his fate. Finally, around midnight, Marvis heard the familiar squeal of his father's Corvette coming up the driveway. His mother had also been waiting up to greet her husband. Marvis began praying that she would have amnesia or something. He heard his father come in and then the usual question, "What do I need to know, honey?" "Well," his mom replied, "there were a few bills in today's mail, and there was a phone call for you this morning." "Unbelievable!" Marvis thought, "My prayers are working! Mom has forgotten!" But then his mother continued, "Oh, yes, and Marvis punched Jacquelyn in the stomach." Oh, no! She did remember! Immediately, Marvis heard his dad's footsteps coming toward his bedroom. It sounded like Frankenstein's monster coming up the hall. Desperate, Marvis tried to fake sleep. "Okay you little scamboogah, come out of there, I know you're not sleeping." Hopelessly trapped, Marvis walked out with his hands up.

First there was the lecture. "Marvis," Joe began in a steady but stern voice, "I told you before that you're supposed to be the man of the house. You're supposed to protect your mom and your sisters. That's your job when I'm not home. And now you hit your sister? You're bigger than her – you wanna know what it feels like?"

Then, there was the punishment. "Marvis," his dad paused, then continued, "we're going down to the zoo." Uh oh – The "zoo" was a space in their cellar where, among other sports equipment, there were boxing gloves. In his defense, Marvis started crying, but that wasn't going to commute this "sparring" session.

Once father and son got to the basement, Marvis, still sobbing, put on his gloves, while Joe only put on the left one. Then Joe began. "Why – jab – did – jab – you – jab

– hit – jab – your – jab – sister? When – jab – daddy's – jab – not – jab – home – jab – you're – jab – supposed – jab – to – jab – be – jab – the – jab – man – jab – of – jab – the – jab – house! What's the matter you little sissy, can't you fight?" With that comment, Marvis flailed about wildly for a few seconds, until his father hit him a bit harder and knocked him down. "Now you know what it feels like to be hit by a man," Joe said before warning him, "don't ever hit a woman again!"

The second sparring session that Marvis had with Smokin' Joe Frazier came about seven years later. The year was 1981. Marvis had recently finished his illustrious amateur career and was just starting as a professional. Sports Illustrated magazine wanted to do a cover story about Marvis and Joe Frazier for their June, 1981, issue, so they sent out writers and a photographer to follow the two around as they prepared for Marvis's fourth professional fight. During one session at Joe's gym, the Sports Illustrated people proposed father and son facing each other in the ring for some photographs of them sparring. The two agreed and into the ring they went. Marvis was very confident about his ability, having won the national amateur heavyweight championship the previous year and currently undefeated as a professional. Joe hadn't been in the ring for some time and was probably a bit rusty, so trainer George Benton cautioned Marvis to take it easy on his dad. Nevertheless, Marvis thought this would be a good opportunity to show pop some of his skills. In the first round, following George Benton's suggestion, Marvis took it easy on his dad. As the second round started Joe taunted Marvis with "come on, you can do better than that." Marvis responded by picking up the pace and tagging the "old man" repeatedly. It felt good, and he soon got carried

Chapter 5 After Larry Holmes : Two Strikes, But Not Out

away. Marvis circled his father and laid leather on him again and again. "This is for the time you wouldn't let me go out," Marvis thought as he landed another punch. "And this is for that time I was grounded." As they started a third round of their session, Marvis was feeling high - "high on the hog." Emboldened by his success, he started right where he left off. This round, however, he added a little "Ali shuffle" to his footwork. "And this is for the time ... BAM! Joe's left hook came from out of nowhere and sent Marvis toward the canvas. Thoughtfully, Joe reached out and caught his son before he went down. "You alright, son?" he asked a stunned Marvis. The chip off the old champ could not answer at that moment, but it was clear he had been brought back to his senses.

Meanwhile, back in the year 1984, Marvis had put in enough time in the gym and done enough sparring that Joe felt he was ready for another fight. It had been almost a year since Marvis fought Holmes, so his dad started him out easy by picking David Starkey as his opponent. Although Starkey, 6'5", had fought both James "Buster" Douglas and Carl "The Truth" Williams, his record was only three wins and seven losses, and he was generally considered no match for Marvis. On September 25, 1984, Marvis took less than three minutes to turn that opinion into fact, when he overwhelmed David Starkey for a TKO in the first round.

Over the next year, Marvis would take on and easily defeat four more challengers, all tough and all with winning records. There was Bernard Benton, who as a cruiserweight (and eventual WBC title holder in that weight class) took his sixteen and one record and stepped up to the heavyweight class to fight Marvis on October 23, 1984. There was the undefeated (fourteen and zero)

Nigerian boxer, Funso Banjo, who was another of the big boxers Marvis had to face in his career. Marvis gave him his first loss on December 5, 1984. In May of 1985, Marvis corralled James "Cowboy" Tillis in a ten round unanimous decision. Tillis was known as a very talented fighter with great potential. He had won his first twenty matches and was thirty-one and five at the time Marvis tangled with him. James Tillis also had the distinction of being the first fighter to go the distance against Mike Tyson. Interestingly, Tillis had Marvis on the ropes and in trouble in the second round of their fight, but referee Joey Curtis gave Marvis a standing eight count, and Marvis survived the round and recovered in his corner after the round ended. The situation was similar to the Holmes fight, when Marvis was hurt and pinned in the corner at the end of their first round. In that fight, the standing eight count was also available, but referee Mills Lane failed to use it. For his final fight that year, Marvis took on another tall and tenacious boxer named Jose Ribalta in September of 1985. Ribalta was 6'5" and had a nineteen and two record. Less than a year later, Ribalta would give Mike Tyson his best fight during Tyson's undefeated years, going toe to toe with him for nine rounds before referee Rudy Battle questionably stopped the fight half way through the tenth. On this night in September, Marvis Frazier and Jose Ribalta would go toe to toe for all ten rounds. Two of the three judges saw Marvis as the winner in this close battle, while the third saw it as even, giving Marvis the majority decision win. It was now late 1985, and Marvis had won five in a row since the October, 1983, loss to Larry Holmes. His position as a contender for another title shot was improving greatly. The WBC had him ranked #10 in the world. One more big win might do it. Marvis needed that win to be against

Chapter 5   After Larry Holmes : Two Strikes, But Not Out

another big name fighter, someone ranked in the top ten. Enter James "Bonecrusher" Smith.

James "Bonecrusher" Smith was aptly nicknamed. He was 6'4", weighed two hundred and thirty-five pounds, and was a powerful puncher with either hand. Smith had lost his first professional fight to James Broad but then won the next fourteen matches in a row, twelve of them by knockout. In the four fights before meeting Marvis, Smith had a close win over Jose Ribalta, and close losses to Larry Holmes, Tony Tubbs, and Tim Witherspoon. Bonecrusher's fifteen and four record, along with his huge potential landed him the WBC's #8 ranking in the world. Marvis and James Smith were not strangers, they had fought as amateurs and sparred at Joe Frazier's Gym.

The fight, arguably the second most important of young Frazier's professional career up to that point, took place in Richmond, California, on February 23, 1986. It was important enough to be broadcast by CBS television network. The announcers were Tim Ryan and Gil Clancy.

After a shaky first round, during which Smith landed several big blows, Marvis found his groove in the second. From that point on he was a busy boxer, scoring repeatedly and demonstrating superior foot speed. As announcer Gil Clancy pointed out, this frustrated Smith and won Marvis several rounds in a row. Bonecrusher responded by focusing on his left jab and trying to set up one big punch. Marvis mitigated that strategy by slipping nearly every jab and countering with lefts of his own. In the fifth round, Marvis was in control of the fight and receiving glowing compliments from both announcers. Then with only seconds left in the round, Smith caught Frazier with a hard right. He followed up with a left that scored, then dropped Marvis with a bone crushing right to the jaw.

Marvis jumped right up to show that he wasn't hurt, but the truth was that the big right from "Bonecrusher" Smith had severely dislocated his jaw. Fortunately, the bell rang to end the round only seconds later.

In his corner, Marvis's cousin, Rodney, could see that the jaw was damaged and pleaded with Joe to stop the fight. Through clenched teeth, Marvis insisted that it go on. He knew how important this fight was and felt sure he could win – so, go on it did. In the sixth round, Marvis kept Smith on the defensive, pressing forward with combinations that scored heavily. However, by the seventh round the pain in the jaw was intensifying, and Marvis had to fall back to a defensive posture to protect it. Regardless, by that time Bonecrusher was nearly spent and wasn't able to mount a significant attack. The announcers were not aware of the injured jaw and complained when the tempo of the fight dropped off in the later rounds. Tim Ryan commented on how important this fight was given that the winner could well find himself in title contention, yet neither fighter seemed to be fighting with that in mind. It was easy for them to see that Smith was tired, but what was up with Frazier? For the final four rounds the slow pace dragged on, as Marvis protected his jaw from another big punch, and Smith was too exhausted to throw one. At the end, Gil Clancy and Tim Ryan thought that the fight was up for grabs, but the judges saw it clearly for Frazier, giving him the win by unanimous decision. When the referee raised Marvis's arm in victory, it was easy to see the now swollen jaw and pain in his eyes. Yet, Marvis had his big win and a second title shot was now within his grasp – though first he had this new injury to contend with.

Just two months after Marvis defeated James "Bonecrusher" Smith to move closer to his hoped for re-match with Larry Holmes, Michael Spinks captured a split decision victory over Holmes in their re-match,

Chapter 5 After Larry Holmes : Two Strikes, But Not Out

and Larry failed to regain the heavyweight title. Seven months earlier, Spinks had become the first reigning light-heavyweight champion to win the heavyweight title (and kept Larry Holmes from tying Rocky Marciano's career undefeated record), with an upset of Holmes in a close but unanimous decision win. By defeating "Bonecrusher" Smith, Marvis had increased his chances of another title shot, but since Spinks had beaten Holmes twice, that shot would not be against Larry Holmes. In early 1986, Joe Frazier had several options to consider for the continuation of his son's boxing career, but none of them included a re-match with Larry Holmes to win the heavyweight championship and erase the shame that Marvis felt about how he had "messed up" in their first fight.

When Marvis was asked twenty-five years later what he was thinking about at that time regarding his boxing career options, he responded, "I can't really remember what I was thinking at that time. I just know that I was in a fog about what was going to happen next."

Marvis contemplates the next step for his career.
(Photo Courtesy of Webster Riddick)

Chapter 6

Wounded Warrior

"Marvis was injury prone." (a statement made by Joe Frazier in chapter 9 of his book, Smokin' Joe: The Autobiography)

Fortunately for Marvis, his injured jaw looked (and felt) worse than it really was. Everyone assumed that it was broken, but upon examination of the injury, Frazier family orthopedist, Joseph Fabiani realized that the jaw was only dislocated, and although it was severe, Dr. Fabiani was able to successfully restore it without surgery. Dr. Fabiani's success shortened the recovery time for Marvis and allowed him to get back to the gym quickly. Such was not always the case with injuries that Marvis suffered during his career.

Boxing is a brutal contact sport. Although it has been made more civil by the acceptance of a modernized version of the Marquees of Queensbury Rules,[2] the very goal of the contest and the path to victory is to punch your opponent more than he punches you, or to punch your opponent so hard that he is unable to continue. Naturally, every punch that connects causes pain, and some blows cause injury. Injuries can also occur from the mere physical exertion in a boxing match or in the practice required to prepare for a match. Like all contact sports, most of the injuries that occur in boxing are minor and go unnoticed. Some, however, are serious enough to require medical attention

---

(2) - *A code of 12 rules for the sport of boxing published in 1867 by Englishman John Graham Chambers, emphasizing sportsmanship and fair play.*

and can possibly even threaten the boxer's career. Marvis Frazier has had his share of these.

Ironically, but probably not unusual for the boxing profession, most of the serious injuries that Marvis experienced took place during training and not during matches. This makes sense considering the large amount of training time allocated to sparring and although sparring is usually not as intense as the fighting that occurs in matches, the stories that boxers tell about memorable sparring sessions reveal that tempers can flare and bad things can happen. Marvis labeled his sparring sessions with Micheal Spinks as "wars," the result of two talented and very competitive fighters in the ring together. What a great match those two could have had, but no such match was ever arranged. So, a couple of sparring sessions was as close as the two would ever get to battling it out. Naturally, they fought hard in these two "practice" sessions. The outcome of one of these "wars" was a hard punch flush to the chest of Frazier, resulting in a cracked sternum. A cracked sternum is painful, of course, but more importantly, Marvis needed over two weeks of inactivity to let the breastbone mend. The dislocated jaw, an injury that did occur in a match, required a similar amount of downtime. Dr. Fabiani used his expertise to reset the jaw but then wired it shut temporarily to insure that the harm done by the dislocation would heal. Marvis begrudged the two weeks of training time lost but got a kick out of eating all of his meals with a straw (lots of soup!).

These two injuries were painful and required some recuperation time but were nothing compared to the three other serious injuries Marvis sustained, all of which threatened his career, including one that could have left him disabled for life.

One of the biggest injury risks that a professional boxer faces is an injury to one of his eyes. Marvis experienced serious injuries to both. In his left eye, Marvis suffered a torn retina and in his right eye, a detached retina. Both injuries required medical treatment to correct and both required down time for recuperation, but the detached retina threatened his career and damaged his eye sight for life.

A torn retina and a detached retina are similar injuries. Both involve the light-sensitive tissue lining the inside back of the eye, known as the retina. Light rays entering the eye ball strike the retina, where they are converted into impulses and passed on to the optic nerve. If the eye was a camera, the retina would be equivalent to the film inside the camera (though much more complicated). Blunt trauma to the eye can cause a tear in this tissue, when the clear gel material that fills the eye (the vitreous) squishes from the blow to the eye ball itself and actually pulls at the retina as it moves away so quickly. The severity of the injury depends on the size of the tear (or tears) and how soon the eye receives treatment following the event.

Marvis was lucky with the torn retina in his left eye. It happened during a sparring session, and Marvis was immediately aware that an injury had occurred. The session was halted, and Marvis was sent to the ophthalmologist. As for treatment, it was decided that the tearing of the retina in his left eye was minor enough that a patch and some time off from physical activity would be enough to get Marvis back in the ring, with no negative consequences to his sight.

Marvis was not so lucky, however, with the injury to his right eye. Less than two years after the torn retina in his left eye, Marvis was again hit hard in the eye during a sparring session. Unfortunately, this time the blow was a thumb delivered directly to the eye ball with tremendous force. Instantly, the sight in his right eye went to a blur. An examination revealed the worst. The surface of the retina had torn dramatically and vitreous material had been forced through the tear in behind the retina. Like old wall paper that has lost its adhesion, the retina peeled away from the inside back of the eye. This condition can result in blindness, so surgery was performed on Marvis to re-attach the retinal lining to the inside back of his eye and repair the tear. After the surgery, it was several months of wait and see – literally. Would Marvis get his sight back in that eye? Would he be able to fight again? Marvis put his trust in God's will for his life. When the recovery time was up, Marvis did indeed have the sight restored in his right eye and he was able to climb back into the ring to continue his pursuit of the heavyweight title, but his eyesight would never be the same. To this day, Marvis wears a contact lens to help make up for the loss of sight he suffered from that blow.

Not long after his right eye was healed enough for Marvis to return to the ring, the warrior was wounded once again. And once again, he was injured during a practice session. Back at his dad's gym, following recuperation from his eye surgery, Marvis moved cautiously while regaining his previous physical condition. Eventually, after a few weeks of workouts, Marvis climbed back into the ring to begin sparring again. The concern was the eye and the less than perfect vision he now had in that eye. Neither was a problem. Shortly after returning to full workouts, Marvis looked just like his former self: dancing around his sparring partners, ducking, blocking, and slipping punches, then countering with barrages of punches of his own. Marvis looked good and he felt good too, confident

Chapter 6   Wounded Warrior

now that he could get back to pursuing the heavyweight championship. NOT SO FAST. One afternoon, Marvis was sparring with top ranked boxer Pinklon Thomas in preparation for his next bout. Thomas was a tough fighter with an excellent jab, but the former WBC heavyweight champion was a respectful fighter and thoughtful partner for sparring. Marvis was moving to slip one of those great Pinklon Thomas jabs when it happened. There was a sound like a cap gun. Marvis stepped back on his right foot, then collapsed. Lying on the canvas, Marvis knew he had another serious injury. The pain was severe, he couldn't move his right foot, and the swelling had already begun. His father, who was watching the sparring session, had seen Marvis go down without being hit, thought he was goofing around, and ordered him to get up. When Marvis claimed he couldn't move his leg, Joe took one look at his son's right foot and could see that there was no goofing around going on. Marvis was injured and needed Dr. Fabiani again.

Joseph Fabiani, M.D. recognized a ruptured Achilles tendon when he saw one. Marvis was admitted to the hospital that same day. Apparently Marvis hyper-flexed his ankle joint when he moved to dodge the quick jab from Pinklon Thomas, though Marvis himself felt that by improperly loosening up that day, he set the stage for the injury. Regardless, Marvis would require treatment. The Achilles tendon is the strong, thick tendon that connects the calf muscle to the back of the ankle bone. A tear of the Achilles tendon may be partial or complete and interferes with the movement of the foot, making it impossible to walk properly. Following a more thorough examination of the injury, Dr. Fabiani determined that Marvis had a partial rupture that would be best treated by complete immobilization. This conservative method of treatment avoids the risks of surgery but is believed to be slightly more likely to result in a re-rupture. The treatment consists of restriction of the foot and lower leg in a plaster cast for six to eight weeks, followed by a restriction of stressful physical activities (NO Boxing!) for an additional six to eight weeks after the cast is removed (crutches anyone?). In total, Marvis lost another four or five months of his boxing career, but, because of the skill of Dr. Fabiani, Marvis was able to return to that career and has never had any trouble with his Achilles tendon since.

It is interesting to note that despite the rash of serious injuries that Marvis endured during his professional career, he had almost no injuries as an amateur, even though that part of his career spanned five years and a total of fifty-eight fights. Marvis was also spared many of the minor injuries that are common in the boxing profession. He never had sprained ankles, cracked or broken ribs, facial cuts, or problems with his hands. Even with his injuries as a professional, Marvis always rebounded and returned to the ring and except for reduced vision in his right eye, Marvis never suffered any long term consequences from them, regardless of their seriousness or how likely they were to cause prolonged or re-occurring damage. This was especially the case with the most severe injury of his life.

When you meet Marvis Frazier, you may notice a long, thick scar that starts at the base of his skull, runs down the back of his neck, and stops about where the collar of his shirt begins. If you surmise that this pronounced scar is the consequence of some serious boxing injury, your guess would only be part of the story. A birth defect was the cause, a hidden, dangerous birth defect, but it was boxing that brought the defect to light. Here is the whole story.

Chapter 6 Wounded Warrior

When Marvis was in school, he competed in and excelled at many different sports. Before he dedicated himself to the sport of boxing, he wrestled and he played basketball, baseball, and football. It was in football that he got his first hint of a problem that was lurking in his otherwise athletic physique. Marvis remembers one particular play where he tackled a big running back incorrectly, using his head as a battering ram to bring the opponent down. Of course, the collision was painful, but there was something else. Marvis felt stunned in a way he never had before. There were no complications though, and the incident was tucked away in the back of his memory. Several years later, after Marvis had given up his pursuit of other sports to concentrate on boxing, he got a second warning that all was not well with his body. In an amateur match with Mitch "Blood" Green, Marvis felt his entire left side go numb after taking a big hit. Since the feeling only lasted for several seconds, Marvis, again, didn't give it much thought. Something was stirring however, and not long after the Mitch Green fight it surfaced again.

In the 1980 Olympic trials, Marvis, the American amateur heavyweight champion, was favored to win the heavyweight position on the United States team. After winning easily in the early levels of the Olympic trials, Marvis was matched up against James Broad in the semi-final stage. The fight never made it past the opening round. James Broad delivered an overhand right punch that hit Marvis in the forehead as he was ducking down and preparing to throw a counter punch. Although it was not a hard hit, Marvis found himself falling to the canvas while still fully conscious. Once he was down, Marvis realized he was unable to move. It took nearly fifteen minutes for the paralysis to pass, and when it did, it was replaced by a "pins and needles" feeling all over his body. The event should have been the wake up call to Marvis and his crew that he had a serious physical problem, but the loss and resulting elimination from the chance at an Olympic Gold Medal overshadowed the strange but "temporary" injury. Incredibly, nearly a year and two professional fights would pass before proper attention was paid to this serious condition.

By the fall of 1980, Marvis had become a professional boxer. On his birthday, September 12, 1980, he had his first fight and gained his first win. One month later, Marvis fought and won again. Returning to his dad's gym to begin training for fight number three, Marvis and Joe finally got the message that there was a serious problem and something had to be done. Fortunately, it was not too late. The final incident took place while Marvis was sparring with the very accomplished Jimmy Young. Young was a great athlete, but he was not a hard hitter. So everyone in the gym was surprised when a jab thrown by Jimmy Young sent Marvis to the canvas. "Get up son!" Joe Frazier barked at Marvis. But Marvis could not get up – he couldn't even move. Again, like in the Olympic trials, he lay on the canvas ... paralyzed. Joe was now sure that Marvis had a serious problem and it wasn't temporary. Finally, attention would be paid.

Following this severe episode of paralysis at the gym, Marvis was taken to Dr. Fabiani's office, where Dr. Fabiani performed some simple tests using physical manipulation and immediately recommended neurosurgeon Frederick Simeone. Dr. Simeone was a renowned neurosurgeon who practiced in Philadelphia and had participated in the writing of several books about the spine and spinal surgery. Marvis was rushed to his office. Upon hearing the details of the injury, Dr. Simeone was able to make a swift diagnosis. Marvis suffered from Spinal Congenital Stenosis.

Marvis was born with a limited width of the spinal canal in his neck. Inactive people with this birth defect can live their entire lives without incident or detection, but an athlete with Spinal Congenital Stenosis, especially in a sport like boxing, is at grave risk of spinal cord injuries. Pinching or bruising of the spinal cord within the unusually narrow canal, caused by the neck being forced too far forward or backward or compressed, as was the case for Marvis, by a blow to the head, can cause transient quadriplegia, a temporary loss of movement in both arms and legs. Severe or repeated bruising of the spinal cord can even end in permanent paralysis. Marvis was lucky to have avoided such an outcome, and he was also lucky to have Dr. Simeone as his surgeon – the man who literally wrote the book *(Posterior Cervical Spine Surgery)* on the necessary surgery (laminectomy).

A laminectomy was the surgical procedure that Dr. Simeone performed on Marvis. It involves entering the spinal column area through the back of the neck to remove the vertebral bone known as the lamina. This increases the space for the spinal cord and greatly reduces the chance of additional pinching or bruising. Amazingly, nothing is put back in to replace the bone material that has been removed. The thick muscle tissue and tendons on the back of the neck are sufficient, even for an athlete to return to a contact sport like boxing. Certainly this was the case for Marvis, who went on to fight nineteen times after his surgery and never again suffered any symptoms.

Incidentally, while Marvis was recuperating for several months after his laminectomy and wondering if he would be able to continue his boxing career, he counseled with his surgeon. Dr. Simeone assured Marvis that the procedure was done properly, it was healing nicely, and it would be safe for him to return to boxing. However, Dr. Simeone advised Marvis not to. He saw boxing as a brutal sport with risk of negative neurological consequences. Dr. Simeone also viewed Marvis as someone who had many opportunities before him. He didn't have to be a professional boxer to go far in life. Marvis graciously thanked Dr. Simeone and told him he would pray about it. Four months later, Marvis was ready to fight again. Dr. Simeone reluctantly provided him with a release to do so.

In 2011, while being interviewed about the injuries he suffered during his boxing career, Marvis was asked if he thought of himself as injury prone. He answered without any hesitation, "No."

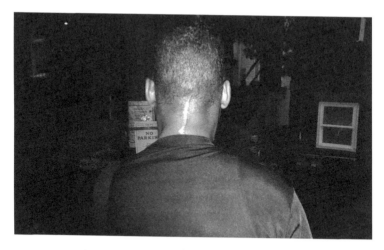

*Ominous reminder of what could have been.
(Photo Courtesy of Marvis)*

Chapter 7

Mike Who?

*"As I stood in the ring waiting for the start of the fight, I could hear the sound of the crowd. It was just background noise, but I could also hear individual voices: the referee, the announcer, my cousin cheering for me from his ringside seat. When the fight started, the sound of the crowd got louder. I threw one jab. Then we moved into the corner. I didn't see the uppercut coming, but suddenly the sound of the crowd stopped; it was quiet, silent, even peaceful. The next thing I remember, I was lying on the canvas in the corner. The referee was asking me if I was alright. I said, 'Yes, sir.' He told me I'd better stay still for a couple of seconds, then he asked me if I knew where I was. I said, 'No, I don't know where I am.' He asked me if I was in the Catskills. I said, 'Yes.' Then he asked me what I was doing there. I answered, 'Well, I **was** fighting Mike Tyson.'* (Marvis Frazier talking about the only time he was knocked unconscious in seventy-nine fights as a boxer)

Mike Tyson - the most ferocious fighter in the history of boxing? The most devastating puncher to ever put on gloves? An Animal in the ring? The baddest man on the planet? The best heavyweight boxer of all time? All matters of opinion – subjects for never ending discussion among boxing aficionados ... but by July 26, 1986, there were four known facts about "Iron Mike." 1. Mike Tyson had just turned twenty years old (born in Brooklyn, New York, on June 30, 1966). 2. Mike Tyson had become a professional only seventeen months earlier, but during those seventeen months he had fought twenty-four times. 3. Mike Tyson had won all twenty-four of those fights, twenty-two by knockout, with fourteen of those knockouts delivered in the first round. 4. Mike Tyson was ranked by the World Boxing Council (WBC) as the #2 heavyweight contender in the world, only seventeen months after his professional debut.

There is no disputing that Mike Tyson was a professional boxing phenom in the mid 1980's. While so many good heavyweight boxers were vying for the rightful claim to the Joe Frazier, George Foreman, Muhammad Ali, Larry Holmes championship lineage, Cus D'Amato, Jim Jacobs, and Kevin Rooney were grooming their "Dynamite Kid," Mike Tyson, for the role. What made Mike's legal guardian and manager, Cus D'Amato, so sure that Mike was the next great heavyweight? Although he was only five feet, ten inches tall, Tyson had great strength and outstanding hand speed, timing, and coordination. His punches were accurate, powerful, and thrown with what D'Amato labeled "bad intentions."

When the management/training trio threw open the laboratory doors and unleashed their "monster" at the professional boxing world on March 6, 1985, walls began to fall, castles began to crumble, and the heavyweight scramble to the top was a whole different game. Tyson, averaging more than a fight a month, moved quickly up the ranks, mowing down one opponent after another in spectacular fashion. After thirteen months, Mike had nineteen fights, nineteen wins, and nineteen knockouts. Three months later, he had five more fights, five more wins, and three more KO's. It was midway through July, 1986, and time for Tyson to tackle some top ranked contenders. The Tyson team was eyeing a title fight by the end of the year and needed a tougher opponent to test their "Dynamite Kid." Marvis Frazier had just defeated James "Bonecrusher" Smith in February and was ranked as the #9 heavyweight contender in the world by the WBC. The Mike Tyson machine trained its sights on this worthy opponent.

Marvis Frazier was, himself, only twenty-five. Over the previous fourteen months he had beaten James Tillis, Jose Ribalta, and "Bonecrusher" Smith to move up in the rankings and re-position himself as a fighter worthy of a second shot at the title. Mike Tyson, who was all the rage in the media because of the devastating knockouts he had afforded so many of his opponents, was ranked as the number two contender. A win by Marvis over Tyson would have been considered an upset but would almost certainly propel Marvis to the number one heavyweight contender position and another shot at the title.

As for the chances of that upset win taking place, many boxing authorities and sportswriters agreed with ABC TV commentator and boxing expert, Alex Wallau, who felt that it wasn't a matter of if Mike Tyson would knock Marvis Frazier out in the fight, but when. Wallau told fellow commentator, Jim Lampley, that Marvis had talent and was a heavyweight fighter to be contended with but that his style made him a perfect target for a bomber like Mike Tyson.

On the other hand, there were some who felt that Marvis had the boxing skills to hold off Tyson long enough to tire him out and frustrate him, eventually outscoring him for a decision victory. It is interesting to note, that the only two opponents who had gone the distance against Tyson in his twenty-four fights up to that point in his career, James Tillis and Mitch Green, were both boxers whom Marvis had beaten. As for handling big hitters, Marvis had never really been knocked out in seventy-five fights (as a professional and amateur). His knockout loss to James Broad in the 1980 Olympic trials was the result of the paralysis caused by his neck injury, not the punch thrown by Broad. Also his 1983 loss to Larry Holmes in his first title fight was a technical knockout. Marvis was still standing and fully conscious when the fight was stopped, even after taking several hard shots to the head from Holmes. Finally, Marvis had just defeated James "Bonecrusher" Smith in his previous fight, a big, strong, hard hitter who was nicknamed "Bonecrusher" for a reason.

The fight, itself, took place on July 26, 1986, in Glens Falls, New York. The event played to a packed house at the Glens Falls Civic Center and was also broadcast on ABC Sports. Marvis, who entered the ring first, did not show the fear that many of Tyson's opponents had. Instead, Marvis faced Tyson's corner with a look of disdain. When Mike Tyson entered the ring as the favored fighter and favorite son, he was jocular, almost jovial and characteristically wearing black trunks with no robe and no socks. He wandered around the ring like he couldn't wait to get it on with Marvis.

Once the fight was underway, the two fighters came quickly together near center ring. Tyson started the punching, throwing a couple of rights that Marvis easily slipped, then several left jabs that Marvis blocked as he backed up toward the ropes. Tyson repeated the series, and Marvis again slipped the rights and blocked the jabs, but this time he threw out a left jab of his own and moved

Chapter 7 Mike Who?

toward the corner. Tyson followed him in and fired off three more quick left jabs. Now Marvis was precariously positioned in the corner, his back against the ropes. Mike Tyson planted himself and with an effort that seemed to focus every muscle in his body into his right fist, drove an uppercut between Marvis's closed elbows and into his chin. No further blows were necessary at that point, because Marvis was "out on his feet." But the Mike Tyson fighting machine was programmed to put a man down, and he blasted Marvis with three more powerful punches, sending him to the canvas. Referee Joe Cortez moved in to start the ten count, but by the count of five he realized that Marvis was unconscious and called the fight off so that the downed fighter could be attended to. Mike Tyson, at first, ran over to have a closer look at his twenty-third knockout victim, but when Marvis seemed to be coming to, Mike rushed back to center ring to leap in the air and gesture to the crowd, celebrating this huge triumph over his best opponent to date.

Mike Tyson supposedly said that everyone has a plan until they get hit. For Marvis Frazier in his fight against Mike Tyson, his plan was simple – to use the supreme self confidence he had acquired as the son of Smokin' Joe Frazier to continue a family fighting legacy second to none. Marvis had great confidence in his ability, no matter who his opponent, to "get the job done." Mike who? Mike Tyson? Well, I'm gonna show you who I am. I'm Marvis Frazier. And then he got hit.

Years later, Mike Tyson was convicted of rape in Indianapolis, Indiana, and sentenced to serve a six year term in what is now called the Plainfield Correctional Facility. When Marvis Frazier heard about Mike's fate, he sent him a letter of encouragement. Later, while Mike was still incarcerated, Marvis, now retired from boxing, was traveling with an organization founded by Chuck Colson called Prison Fellowship. At one point in their travels, the Prison Fellowship people visited prisons in Indiana, including a stop at the Plainfield Correctional Facility. Mike Tyson refused to come out, but when word was sent that Marvis Frazier was part of the visiting group, Mike asked for permission to go see him. The two met at the gate, where they talked for fifteen or twenty minutes. Mike thanked Marvis for the letter he had sent, and Marvis prayed for Mike. Finally, when their time was up, the two parted. Marvis Frazier rejoined the other Fellowship members and Mike Tyson rejoined the other prisoners.

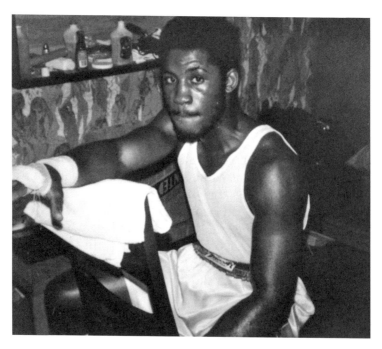

(Photo Courtesy of Darryl Lee)

Chaper 8

Retirement

"Pop always said that when boxing feels like a job, it is time to do something else."

In his fight against Mike Tyson, Marvis was knocked out and completely unconscious but recovered very quickly. After the first uppercut, Marvis was "out on his feet," but Tyson belted him with three more debilitating punches as he collapsed to the canvas. However, only seconds later Marvis was awake and answering questions from the referee. Within two minutes, Marvis was standing and being embraced by members of both corners.

Marvis made his way back to the Frazier dressing room, where the mood was somber. The members of Marvis's crew were shocked at what had happened in the ring. Marvis, himself, was stunned. The room was deathly silent. The ring doctor slipped in quietly to have a closer look at Marvis. He concluded that Marvis had no permanent physical damage from the beating he had taken and quickly departed. Marvis was the first to break the renewed silence when he spoke to his dad.

"I'm sorry Pop. I didn't measure up," Marvis sullenly told Smokin' Joe.

"Don't worry about it son. All you can do is what you can do," was the stoic response from the boxing icon. "You trained, you went out there, you did everything you were supposed to do; what else can you do?"

Val Colbert, who was both a trainer and good friend

to Marvis, tried to console the grieving fighter. With the long, strong arm of a former wrestler draped gently over both of Marvis's shoulders, Val pulled himself within a whisper's distance of the young man and repeated the well worn truism of competition. "All you can do is what you can do, man. You did your best. All you can do is what you can do."

Nothing anyone said really helped ... not after he lost ... not after he lost big. Marvis, who absolutely expected to defeat Mike Tyson, had very little experience with losing, but even as distraught as he was with this stunning loss, he had the wisdom to know that "You can't cry the blues when you lose, because you're grinning when you're winning." Marvis finished changing and left the dressing room for a short press conference where he politely answered every question before sequestering himself in his motel room for the night.

Marvis slept that night like a man overcome with fever, tossing and turning, his dreams mere moments of thoughts and flashes of feelings. Seconds seemed to tick the time out, but morning finally arrived. Marvis awoke with a start and for a minute, his head was clear of all recent memory – tranquil. He was undefeated again and soon to challenge for the heavyweight championship of the world. He smiled. Daralyn's voice brought him crashing back to earth.

"You okay, honey?" His young wife asked from the opposite side of the king sized bed.

Marvis gingerly passed his fingers across his face and under his chin before responding.

"Yeah, I'm alright," he replied slowly, meaning, of course, only physically. Already, the memories of the fight and the onerous feelings that followed were flowing back into his head like an incoming tide. On the outside Marvis looked fine, but inside his head, questions and doubt were crowding out all other thoughts.

"How did this happen?" "What did I do wrong?" "How did this guy beat me like that?" For Marvis there was total disbelief.

Daralyn began to tidy up the motel room so that they could start for home. Marvis dressed but then sat on the edge of the bed like a statue, frozen in thought.

"Is something wrong here?" "Am I in the right game?" "Is the Lord trying to tell me something?" His disbelief began turning to self doubt.

It was now mid morning, and Daralyn suggested that they get started. Although the couple was traveling by limousine, it would take nearly six hours to reach Philadelphia, and they both just wanted to get home.

Once back in Philly, Marvis barely felt up to it and dragged his feet some but eventually forced himself back into the gym. Within a week of the fight he walked through the doors at Joe Frazier's but with his head hanging low and an apology on his lips. Marvis apologized to everybody, the staff, the trainers, and the other boxers. He felt that he had let everyone down and wanted desperately to make it up to them, but he didn't know how. For now, all Marvis could do was apologize.

Things weren't good. For months Marvis sleep walked through practice. During his sparring sessions, punches were landing against him that had never gotten through before. Marvis was listless and moped around both in and out of the gym. There was talk. What's up with Frazier? What's going on with Marvis? It was just talk though. Everyone knew that Marvis was struggling with the loss to Tyson, trying to figure out what he did wrong, trying to figure out how it happened the way it did, trying to figure out what was next for him in boxing.

Finally, after Marvis had suffered with this state of mind for more than six months, Smokin' Joe approached his son about fighting again. Marvis hesitated. For the first time in his boxing career, he entertained the fear of failure. Wisely, Smokin' Joe was considering an opponent for Marvis well below his caliber. Even so, Marvis still feared the worst. What if a lesser boxer beat him? Most critics had attributed his loss to Holmes to inexperience. Mike Tyson had, since their fight, crushed three more opponents, captured the WBC heavyweight title, and was proving himself unbeatable. But no one would excuse Marvis for a loss to a journeyman or a club fighter.

Still, Marvis felt he had to make an effort. He had to try to get his career back on track. "Okay, Pop. Let's give it a shot," he told his dad on an early spring day, setting in motion his return to the ring.

Tom Fischer was a journeyman fighter. He was several years older than Marvis, having started his professional career in the mid 1970's. Fischer had won thirty-four of his forty-four fights and had fought some big name fighters over the years, but none of his wins had come against any of them (though he had beaten one poor chap six times in six meetings!). His fight with Marvis was to be his last and what a memorable way to go out – defeating a high profile boxer like Marvis Frazier.

Of course, it was not to be. Marvis, showing the boxing skills that had taken him so far in the sport, pummeled Tom Fischer into submission, putting him down twice in the second round and forcing referee Vincent Rainone to call the fight. Afterward, as he was being congratulated by his corner, Marvis felt much better. "Yeah, I guess I've still got it," he told Val Colbert on their way back to the dressing room.

After this success and while Marvis was feeling a bit better about his boxing, Joe thought that another match should be arranged as soon as possible. So, just over two months later, a second fight was scheduled for Marvis, again at the Hilton in Secaucus, New Jersey. This time, Marvis was matched against Robert Evans, an imposing fighter who, like Tom Fischer, had battled many big names in the fight game. Though Evans had not managed any wins against the better heavyweights, he usually fought well and scored a couple of draws and several close losses. Marvis was unable to knock Robert Evans out but dominated the ten round fight for a unanimous decision. After this second consecutive victory, Marvis's record stood at eighteen wins, with only two losses, and his boxing career seemed to be getting back on track.

Unfortunately, Marvis was still in a fog. Despite two fine performances since the loss to Tyson and his outstanding overall record to bank on, Marvis felt that something was missing, a spark, a spirit, a feeling. Marvis thought of it as a "presence." This "presence" was something he had felt for most of his career. Marvis reasoned that, like Samson of the Old Testament who had supernatural strength from God for combat and heroic feats, the "presence" he felt was from the Lord. It gave him strength with his battles in and out of the ring, conviction in his goal of winning the heavyweight championship, and confidence in the achievement of that goal.

With the "presence," Marvis was clear headed, determined, focused, and teeming with confidence. Now Marvis began to admit to himself that he didn't feel the same and hadn't for some time. The "presence" had been going out of him, and he had been trying to get it back. It wasn't measured by wins and losses or fight performance, so it couldn't be judged by boxing analysts or experts. The "presence" was a feeling only Marvis could sense, and his sense now was that it was gone. For the first time in his career, Marvis seriously considered retirement.

Retirement was a frightening idea. Marvis was only twenty-seven years old. Since he was fifteen, Marvis had nurtured the dream of winning the heavyweight championship of the world. Returning the title to the Frazier family was the goal of his life. Retirement would mean abandoning that dream and letting go of the chance of achieving that goal. Marvis spent most of the next ten months pondering over and praying about the situation.

Finally, an opportunity opened up, and Marvis made a decision. Smokin' Joe was able to secure an option for Marvis to fight Philipp Brown. Brown was a good boxer on the verge of contention, sporting a record of thirty wins, only two losses, and two draws. His wins column included victories over Jimmy Young and Marvis's own cousin, Rodney Frazier. Ironically, Marvis had fought Philipp Brown as an amateur, beating him in the 1980 National AAU tournament.

Marvis decided to take the fight. He would give it his all and treat the fight as the next logical step in his return to contention. However, win or lose, if the "presence" didn't come back this time, he was just going to let boxing go. Marvis, like Gideon of the Old Testament, was putting out a fleece for guidance.

The fight was held October 27, 1988, in Tucson, Arizona. It was the feature attraction of the night, with boxer Joey "The Kid" Medina and Arizona sports broadcaster Kevin McCabe sharing the blow by blow announcing. Marvis was in control for most of the fight, aggressively keeping the pressure on Brown from the inside, where he threw barrages of body punches and constant combinations. Brown did catch Marvis with a hard right early in the fourth round and followed up with two more rights, but Marvis shook off the assault and controlled the remaining two minutes of the round. In the ninth round Philipp looked spent, and Marvis nearly took him out, though Brown survived that round and managed to land some good parting shots on Marvis in the tenth. As the fight was ending, announcer Joey Medina, who was sure Marvis had the win, stated that if Marvis kept winning fights like this one against good opponents like Philipp Brown, he might get another shot at the title. In the end, it was another win for Marvis Frazier – his nineteenth as a professional, seventy-fifth overall ... and last as a boxer.

Marvis was, of course, happy with the win in his fight against Philipp Brown, but as he went to the Lord in prayer and supplication in the days that followed and searched his heart, he realized that the "presence" had not come back. Marvis finally admitted to himself that being a professional boxer was no longer for him. It wasn't an easy decision. Marvis was only twenty-eight, still in his prime. Marvis had won three fights in a row since his loss to Mike Tyson. His overall record was nineteen wins, two losses, and he was again a contender. So what! Marvis could deal with all of that. It was the dream that made it so hard, the end of his dream ... and what about telling his father?

The next morning Marvis met Daralyn at the breakfast table with the news.
"Hey, honey, I'm retiring," he told her, almost in passing.
"Okay," Daralyn responded, obviously pleased and not too surprised.

Later that same day, Marvis headed over to the gym to take care of telling his dad. Marvis found his Pop sitting alone in the office.

"Pop, I'm done. I'm retiring from boxing."

"Hey, whatever you want to do son," his father replied.

Smokin' Joe appeared calm and, like Daralyn, not really surprised.

Marvis spent the rest of that day on his own, thinking about his life as a boxer. He remembered how he first got the idea of becoming a boxer when he watched his dad and Muhammad Ali fight in the Philippines. He thought about the fun and excitement he had as an amateur, winning all those fights and all those titles. He recalled the nervous energy that he took into his first professional fight, which he almost lost but then came back to win by knockout. He pleasantly reminisced about the great wins he had against so many good opponents as an undefeated professional. Boy, did he have the "presence" in those days! *The "presence" ... hmm; why had he lost it? Why couldn't he get it back? When did it leave him? ... Yes ... yes, he had lost it then.* **The "presence" was no longer there after Larry Holmes.**

The morning after Marvis retired from boxing, he woke up feeling great. His head was clear, and he had a song in his heart. The song was a number one hit by Kool & The Gang and the words go in part, like this:
Celebrate good times, come on!
Let's celebrate.
Celebrate good times, come on!
It's a celebration!

Come on and celebrate, tonight
'Cause everything's gonna be all right.

In style, in the 70's - with (Left to Right) cousins Rodney, Bernard, and friend Ronald (Photo courtesy of Darryl Lee)

Follow me if you like, but don't get near my 1976 Cadillac Seville. (Photos courtesy of Darryl Lee)

Trainers and friends Val Colbert (L) and Sam Hickman (R) with my sister Natasha (Photos courtesy of Darryl Lee)

Later, Val with Pop and my own young girls Tamyra and Tiara. (Photos courtesy of Webster Riddick)

After retirement, should I be ...

A Trainer? *An Announcer?*

A Preacher? *or ...* *A Model?!*

(Photos courtesy of Webster Riddick)

"From the time I was little I loved being a Frazier ... because I loved my family."

Here we are in the mid-1990's (Left to Right), Sisters: Natasha, Jo-Netta, (Me), Weatta, and Jacqui, with Mom and Pop in front.

My Mom, "the Sweet Lady" with me, early 2013

My wonderful sister Jacqui.

(All Photos on this page courtesy of Webster Riddick)

I also have five brothers. Here are: "Rivers," Derek, and Brandon. Hector and "Rubin" are not pictured. (Photo courtesy of Darryl Lee)

And another sister, Renae. (Photo Courtesy of Darryl Lee)

Here's Jacqui again with my cousins (Left to Right) Rodney, Mark, and "cousin" Tyrone. (Photo courtesy of Webster Riddick)

The Fighting Fraziers: sister Jacqui, Pop, and me. We also had brother Hector, and cousins Rodney and Mark join in the fun. (Both Photos on this page are courtesy of Webster Riddick)

Nothing on this Earth...

... beats the love between parent and child.

(All Photos on this page courtesy of Webster Riddick)

And I love my Pop.

(All Photos on this page courtesy of Webster Riddick)

Part II Depression

One ceases to recognize the significance of mountain peaks if they are not viewed occasionally from the deepest valleys.
— Dr. Al Lorin

Chapter 9

It Begins

"That's me! I've got depression!" Marvis exclaimed out loud to himself one weekday afternoon in the mid 1980's while he lay in bed. He was watching television, when he heard a guest on a Maury Povich talk show describe the symptoms of clinical depression - one of which was sleeping or staying in bed more than usual.

For eight years Marvis Frazier had been living a dream come true. From the age of fifteen until age twenty-three, nearly every detail he had imagined in his plan to become a boxer and recapture the heavyweight championship of the world for the Frazier family had happened. The dream started as an adolescent fantasy for Marvis when he tagged along with his Dad to Manilla where Smokin' Joe was going to fight Muhammad Ali for the third time. As Marvis, who was a natural athlete, began to act out his fantasy by participating with his dad's crew as they prepared for the title fight, he exhibited a prowess in boxing consistent with his success in several other sports. Members of the crew noticed and commented. Very quickly, Marvis's fantasy was becoming his dream. He really was going to become a championship boxer, and he knew he could do it.

The strategy necessary to turn a young man's yearnings of achievement into real life success played itself out over the next few years. In this case, it included a commitment to the sport of boxing in exclusion of all other sports and a reordering of life priorities in order to put boxing near the top. For Marvis, these requirements were simply steps he had to take in order to prove his devotion to the dream. Likewise, his continued success and enjoyment of the process were parts of a motivational loop that kept pushing him higher and higher. Before Marvis fought a single bout, the numerous, "Wow! Did you see that?" reactions of his trainers were building within Marvis a sense of confidence, which when combined with the confidence that he already possessed by being a Frazier made Marvis feel invincible.

And indeed, Marvis did appear to be invincible, beginning with a quick knockout in his first ever fight as an amateur and continuing with one convincing victory after another. Cus D'amato is said to have told a young Mike Tyson that the great boxers focused only on winning when they entered the ring. Marvis Frazier never envisioned losing. Why should he? As an amateur, he won his first forty-four fights in a row. When Marvis finally did lose in his fourth year of fighting, it was in a close decision. Marvis graciously accepted the loss, but his confidence was unshaken, because he felt that he had won the fight and had been robbed by the decision.

Even with the surprise loss in the Olympic trials, that Marvis suffered when a James Broad punch sent him to the canvas paralyzed from the neck down, the disappointment was in his failure to make the Olympic team, not in the actual loss itself. Marvis considered that a fluke, not a failure. That loss was caused by the birth defect in his neck - his Spinal Congenital Stenosis. And so, undaunted by his two losses, Marvis marched his way through the amateur ranks with an incredible fifty-six and two record and other than an Olympic gold medal, Marvis won every other major amateur title. His dream was coming true.

Such tremendous success as an amateur further bolstered Marvis's confidence while preparing him for the next level of achievement. On the day of his twentieth birthday, Marvis and his dream took a giant step forward when he joined the ranks of the professionals, and although a bit nervous, he won that fight by knockout. The psychological importance of that win to Marvis could be seen clearly when he uncharacteristically whooped it up in the ring after the fight was over.

As a professional, Marvis continued his winning ways. He defeated one opponent after another just as he had done as an amateur. Smokin' Joe would put up better and better opponents for his son to fight, and Marvis would mow them down. Marvis did face a couple of setbacks as a professional, with his neck surgery and an extended illness, but these were only postponements, not deterrents. With each win in his undefeated professional career, Marvis was getting more sure of the attainment of his goal and his dream was blossoming likewise. By the time he took on and handily defeated the great Joe Bugner, Marvis was on cloud nine. He was at the pinnacle of his dream ... or was it the precipice? Marvis was only twenty-three years old – young for a professional boxer. He had been living his dream come true for eight years. His goal to become a professional boxer and, like his father, win the heavyweight championship of the world had unfolded almost precisely as planned. One more step and the dream would be reality.

When Joe Frazier asked Marvis about a fight with heavyweight champion Larry Holmes, Marvis replied, "Pop, you know I will fight anyone."

When his wife, Daralyn, asked Marvis if he was ready to face the great Larry Holmes, Marvis replied, "Daralyn, you know I can beat anyone."

Marvis went into the November 25th, 1983, battle with Larry Holmes for the championship of the world absolutely certain that he would win. That fight was what he had been working on and thinking about for eight years. The heavyweight championship was his destiny. Winning it would be his dream come true.

He lost. He failed. He "messed up." His dream came crashing down around him. He was devastated.

* * *

Clinical depression can be caused by a single stressful life event. Marvis Frazier's loss to Larry Holmes was so stressful to him, that he was sure no man in the whole world could feel as low as he felt in the ring at that moment. In his mind, he went from the highest high to the lowest low possible. Later, at the hotel room, he drank himself to sleep. When he woke up in the morning, Marvis was at the bottom of a pit so deep that he could not see a way out. Although he didn't know it at that moment, Marvis Frazier had "got depression."

Sadness is a normal reaction to setbacks or disappointments in life. Having the blues or being down in the dumps are feelings anyone can experience after falling short of personal expectations. So it wasn't out of the ordinary for Marvis to feel this way after his loss to Larry Holmes. However, when the sadness persisted day after day, and Marvis began to experience intense feelings of guilt about the loss (he had failed the Frazier family and hadn't lived up to the Frazier name) and feelings of worthlessness because of it, he was likely already dealing with depression. During the eight months that followed his fight with Larry Holmes, Marvis did not return to the gym. Under the guise of taking some time off to "get his head right" and re-focus his thoughts on a new strategy, Marvis stayed at home, where a sense of hopelessness to remedy the situation began to engulf his daily life.

Marvis was confused by the way that he felt. He was a young man who had rarely experienced anything but joy in his life, but was now feeling sorrow, and was surprised by the depth of his distress.

Still, Marvis was sure his feelings were temporary and would soon pass. He decided to keep it all to himself. He and Daralyn spent much of this "time off" looking for a new house as they prepared for the arrival of their first child.

Tamyra was born in the early spring of 1984, several months after the loss to Holmes. She was a beautiful baby, and Marvis was thrilled to be a father. He hoped that the happiness baby Tamyra brought to him and his excitement about being a father would end the gnawing emptiness he had been feeling for months. Marvis focused on his daughter and felt his usual joy of living coming back, but as soon as he thought about returning to the gym he felt down again. He just couldn't muster any interest in the activity that had once given him so much pleasure.

Marvis continued to stay away from the gym, justifying his absence with the need to move his young family into their own house. Nevertheless, as summer approached, rumors began to circulate that his boxing career was over, and Marvis became restless. Then, in June of 1984, Marvis and Daralyn found a home in the Philadelphia suburb of Wyncote. Marvis still had no desire to return to the gym, but with no more excuses and a need to restart his career, he finally returned – eight months after his loss to Larry

Holmes.

For the next two years, Marvis worked to revitalize his career. The quick loss to Holmes had erased any ranking Marvis had before the fight, so he would have to take on and defeat as many top fighters as possible to return to contention. For a skillful boxer like Marvis this strategy was certainly feasible. Yet, how was an athlete in the throes of depression to compete in such a demanding sport at its highest level of competition? After all, boxing is dangerous. Boxers can suffer serious injury, even death in the ring during a fight. Marvis had not only lost interest in the sport that had been the driving force in his life since he was fifteen, but he was also frequently physically fatigued and was having difficulty concentrating. Fortunately, despite these hardships, Marvis found a way to continue.

Marvis fought Larry Holmes in November of 1983. He stayed away from boxing all the following winter and spring. He finally returned to his dad's gym in the summer of 1984. At the time of his return, Marvis knew there was something wrong, but he did not know what it was. "What is wrong with me?" Marvis asked himself over and over, much more like a broken record than an inquiring mind. While in this condition, Marvis discovered autopilot. He became a boxer by rote, everything done by memory and routine. The training was routine. Marvis just had to show up at the gym every day on time and stay until it was over. The matchmaking was routine. Smokin' Joe set up a fight, picked the opponent and Marvis said, "Okay." Even the fighting was routine. "How am I doing, Pop?" Marvis frequently asked his Dad between rounds during his next six fights, revealing his failure to focus and his lack of concentration. Yes, he was even fighting on autopilot.

Amazingly, despite his deepening depression, Marvis

was able to continue to win. In a testament to his boxing skills, Marvis knocked out two hundred thirty-four pound David Starkey in his return to the ring, convincingly defeated sixteen and one fighter Bernard Benton one month later, and manhandled undefeated Funso Banjo a month after that. All the while, he was lacking motivation, fighting fatigue, unable to concentrate, and feeling down in the dumps. After the Banjo fight, Marvis was kept out of commission for a few months by an injury. He returned physically whole but psychologically still damaged. He went on to defeat the highly talented James Tillis and the very tough Jose Ribalta for his fourth and fifth wins in a row. Like an automaton, Marvis responded mechanically to the physical demands of these bouts, but mentally "he just wasn't there." It was incredible that Marvis could continue to box professionally, and win, under these circumstances. Meanwhile, back at his new home with his wife Daralyn ...

At his dad's gym, Marvis was surrounded by others, his trainers, the gym staff, and other fighters, but because of his depression, he felt "empty and all alone." At home, Marvis had Daralyn. Marvis tried to keep his feelings to himself, but Daralyn must have known something was wrong not long after the symptoms started. She would have expected Marvis to be upset about his loss to Holmes, but when his low mood continued for weeks, she probably became worried about him. Finally, after months of moodiness, Marvis opened up to Daralyn and asked her, "What is wrong with me?" Daralyn had no answer for her husband at that time, only continued patience and understanding. It was a question that Marvis would ask his wife many times over the next several years.

As time passed, Marvis became more and more

lethargic at home, as though most of the energy that he had available was expended at the gym, leaving him fatigued, sluggish, and indifferent at the end of each day. Also he was drowsy, very drowsy, so much so, that Marvis spent a lot more time in bed. He wasn't necessarily sleeping, just listlessly lying there with the TV turned on. Ironically, this was the exact setting that would soon start Marvis on a road to recovery. From the mostly meaningless noise of television programming, the voice of a health care professional would reach out during an afternoon talk show and grab Marvis's attention with a description of depression. Once Marvis heard that voice and realized that the answer to his "What is wrong with me?" question was that he "had depression," he would begin to take steps to find a solution, though it would be a long process of trial and error, and he would seem to get worse before he got better. For now, Marvis had more fights to face.

Despite his deepening depression, Marvis had won five straight since his loss to Larry Holmes and was climbing back into contention. Smokin' Joe, who was by now aware that Marvis was struggling emotionally, encouraged his son to keep going and let it work itself out. Joe continued to set up fights that moved Marvis in the direction of another title fight. After the wins over James Tillis and Jose Ribalta in 1985, Joe was able to secure a fight for Marvis against top ten ranked boxer, James "Bonecrusher" Smith in early 1986. A win in this fight could mean a second title shot. Too bad Marvis was still in a fog and was "just not there" for the fight with Smith. However, his skills, training, and conditioning took over again, and Marvis came out on top. Marvis didn't know how he ever won that fight, and he had no idea how he was going to beat his depression.

Chapter 9 It Begins

Not long before his July, 1986, fight with Mike Tyson, Marvis experienced a nightmare that haunted his thoughts for years to come. In the dream, Marvis was on his way home after finishing his time at the gym. When he arrived at home, the house was still. He opened the front door and called out to his wife, but there was no answer. It was dark in the house as there were no lights on and the shades were all drawn. Marvis walked into the large L-shaped living room and turned on the lights. To his amazement, all of the walls in the room were covered with huge mirrors. No matter which way he looked, he saw nothing but blazing distorted reflections of himself. His every movement was reflected a million fold. Marvis tried to get away from the frightening imagery by running out of the room, but every wall in the house was the same, each flooded with light and filled with millions of distorted images of himself. Thoroughly shaken, Marvis called out again for Daralyn. Again, there was no answer, so he rushed for the front door wanting only to get out. Then, as though from some great pressure, the mirrors shattered and began to collapse. An avalanche of glass began to fall all around Marvis. He was being buried alive and could not pull himself out. Marvis cried out for his pop ... then awoke with a start, drenched with perspiration, and gasping for breath.

*Trainer and Friend Val Colbert with Marvis.
(Photo courtesy of Colbert Family)*

Chapter 10

It Ends

    Val Colbert was a trainer for Marvis throughout his boxing career. Val had known Marvis from the time Marvis was a boy, and he was a close friend to him when Marvis became an adult. Upon learning from Marvis about his depression, Val, who was a keen observer of people, made this analogy to try to help his friend through his difficult time:
    "Marvis, take this old gym time sheet and hold it out with both hands. That sheet of paper is your life, your thoughts, your feelings. Now I'm going to set this pencil on top of the paper – that is your wife, Daralyn. This pen is next – that is your baby girl. These erasers are going on now – they are all your bills. Still have a grip on the paper? Here are some coins – your new house. Still got it? These keys are the rest of your family. Can you still hold the weight? Okay. Now this hammer is boxing – look out!" (Val drops the hammer and the old time sheet is torn from Marvis's hands and everything falls to the floor)

    The victory over James "Bonecrusher" Smith was significant for Marvis in his battle back to title contention, but it made little difference in his fight against depression. Even though the win landed Marvis in the # 9 heavyweight contender spot and one or two big wins away from a second shot at the title, his interest, drive, and motivation toward boxing were still lacking. The void this caused affected all areas of his life, robbing Marvis of the joy that he once had in abundance. His depression was a condition, a mood disorder, that although triggered by a stressful event (the failure to win the heavyweight championship), could not be corrected simply by mitigating the result of that stressful event (moving toward a second chance to win the title). Marvis was feeling no better with his sixteen and one record, after beating Smith for his sixth win in a row, than he was with the ten and one record he had right after his loss to Holmes. Fortunately, thanks to a mid-day TV talk show, Marvis at least had an idea what was wrong with him and could pursue a solution.

The first step Marvis took was to open up to other people about what he was experiencing. When the grip of depression first took hold on his life in late 1983, Marvis tried to keep his emptiness and despair completely to himself. However, Daralyn was aware that something was wrong and worried about her husband. After a few months, Marvis let Daralyn in on the question that was spinning through his head when he asked her one day, "What is wrong with me?" After Marvis surmised that he was depressed, he still asked his wife the same question. But now he actually meant, "Why am I depressed, and what can I do about it?" At the gym it was no mystery that Marvis had a problem, but he mostly kept to himself about it, and the other fighters respected his privacy. His dad, however, tried to console him as best he could. He encouraged Marvis to keep going and let things work themselves out. Val Colbert, on the other hand, worked with Marvis often to try to help him understand what was happening to him and why. Val was a wonderful friend to Marvis during his years of depression, and his counseling was a great comfort.

Unfortunately, even after acknowledging his condition and opening up to other people about it, Marvis did not seem to be making any real progress. Even with the help of Daralyn, his dad, and Val, Marvis continued to suffer with the symptoms of depression. This drove him to take further action. For this he used the same TV talk show guest as his source of information. Marvis remembered that the guest had suggested that anyone suffering from the symptoms of depression for more than two weeks should seek help from a professional. Marvis had now been dealing with his depression for more than two years! "Professional" help, to Marvis, meant a psychiatrist. Driven by a desire to make things better, Marvis mustered up the courage to set up an appointment.

Marvis has very little memory and no written records of his "talk therapy" experience. It all happened in the the spring or early summer of 1986. Marvis went to two or three sessions with two different doctors. The first discussed his symptoms with him and determined that Marvis was indeed suffering from clinical depression. Probably, the first doctor recommended the second. It was the second doctor who prescribed medications for Marvis. Marvis has no idea what the medications were, but he distinctly remembers how they made him feel. "Like electricity was going through my body – like sparklers were going off under my skin." Marvis wanted relief from the misery that depression was causing him, but after that reaction, he decided that medication and psychotherapy weren't going to give it to him.

It was the summer of 1986. Marvis was now the proud father of two little girls. Daralyn had given birth to the couple's second child, Tiara, in March. Marvis was ranked #9 in the world by the WBC, and he was scheduled to face heavyweight knockout sensation Mike Tyson in July. Marvis had a chance to erase his loss to Holmes and get his boyhood dream back on track. Yet, Marvis still had clinical depression. Even after recognizing the problem, opening up to others, attending psychotherapy sessions, and trying medication, Marvis faced his fight with Mike Tyson in the same state of mind that he fell into not long after his loss to Larry Holmes. "He just wasn't there."

After his shocking loss to Mike Tyson on July 26, 1986, in Glens Falls, New York, Marvis slipped into an even deeper and more disabling depression. Marvis forced himself back to the gym within a week of the loss but with no desire to fight again. Marvis returned to the gym a broken fighter. For the first time in his career, Marvis had lost confidence in his ability to box.

Marvis did finally fight again. Nearly a year after his loss to Mike Tyson he fought and easily defeated journeyman Tom Fischer and then two months later beat similarly ranked Robert Evans. These two fights gave Marvis back the feeling that he still "had it" as a boxer, but they did little to rekindle his old dream of becoming the heavyweight champion of the world. Instead, Marvis focused on his desire to defeat his depression. This time Marvis turned to his faith in God for the solution. Through prayer and reading the Bible, Marvis realized that he needed to find and follow God's plan for his life if he wanted to gain victory over depression. Marvis faced the possibility that continuing as a professional boxer may no longer be part of God's plan for his life. After all, "the presence" that Marvis had felt throughout the early part of his career had not been with him for years. Was that God's way of telling him something that he didn't want to hear? For the first time in his career, Marvis seriously considered retirement. While he pondered the possibility, Marvis involved himself more and more with the work of the Lord. He spent more time with his family as a good husband to his wife Daralyn and as a father to his two girls. He spent more of his time with church activities, hoping to fulfill his obligations as a member in good standing. And he joined an organization called Prison Fellowship, traveling with a group of Christian athletes and celebrities to prisons around the country. With all this going on, almost a year had passed since his last fight, and Marvis felt that boxing was probably behind him. Still, he wanted to be sure.

Late in the summer of 1988, an opportunity became available for Marvis to determine God's will for his life regarding his boxing career. His dad had signed an option for Marvis to fight Philipp Brown, a boxer whose 30-2-2 record put him on the verge of contention. Marvis decided to take the fight, feeling that it would be a good way to put out a fleece for God's guidance. It wouldn't be winning or losing that Marvis would be testing in this match, but whether "the presence" was there again or not. Win or lose, if "the presence" wasn't there then his boxing career would be over.

Marvis fought Philipp Brown on October 27, 1988. It was a good bout. Both fighters had strong moments, but Marvis controlled most of the action and won a unanimous decision - impressive for a boxer who hadn't fought for nearly fourteen months. In the days after the fight, Marvis prayed and searched his heart, but he knew soon after the fight was over that despite the win, "the presence" had not returned and it was time to retire. The day after Marvis accepted God's will for his life, he told Daralyn and

Smokin' Joe of his decision.

That night he slept soundly and in the morning, miraculously, Marvis woke up full of joy and celebration. His five year battle with depression had ended.

Psalms 30:5... weeping may endure for a night, but joy cometh in the morning.

A few days after Marvis told his wife, Daralyn, that he was retiring from boxing, Daralyn asked, "But won't you miss boxing?"

Marvis answered, "Baby, don't you worry about that. Nothing is more important to me than my Lord and Savior - Jesus Christ, my wonderful wife, and my beautiful daughters."

(Photo courtesy of Webster Riddick)

Part III Loss

*The most beautiful people ... are those who have ... known loss
and have found their way out of (its) depths.
- Elisabeth Kubler-Ross*

*Marvis and Daralyn in the late 1970's.
(Photo courtesy of Darryl Lee)*

Chapter 11

A Storybook Romance ...

Marvis: "Why do you have so many different girl friends?"
Andrew: "Why do I have so many different girl friends?! Because girls are great, man. I love them. You need to get you a few more."
Marvis: "I have Daralyn."
Andrew: "Well, I have Stacy – and she's beautiful too. But I also have Vanessa, ooh-eee!"
Marvis: "I have Daralyn."
Andrew: "Sure, that's good, but I have Alex ... and Joanne ... and Sarah."
Marvis: "I have Daralyn."
Andrew: "Hey, Marvis, the more the merrier. Know what I mean?"
Marvis: "Yeah, I know what you mean, but I have Daralyn. That's all I need and all I want."

(Marvis and his childhood and lifelong friend, Andrew, talking about girls one night when they were both sixteen years old.)

    1976 was an eventful year for Marvis. When the year began, so did his boxing career. By summer, Marvis still hadn't fought his first amateur match, but he was working out in his dad's gym every day. To get to the gym, Marvis had been combining bus and trolley rides with a three block run. But as soon as he hit his sixteenth birthday, which was only a few weeks away, Marvis would be riding in style. Pop had given Marvis his birthday present early, the best he had ever gotten; a shiny blue 1976 Cadillac Seville – the kind of car most sixteen year olds only dream of.

One day, late in the summer of 1976, Marvis and his cousin Bernard were cleaning the Frazier family swimming pool. The job of keeping the pool clean, by vacuuming leaves and dirt lying on the bottom of the pool and skimming debris off the top, was one of the many jobs on a work list given to Marvis by his dad in exchange for a very healthy allowance. But it was one that Marvis had been doing long before the jobs list existed. It was a fun job, and Bernard gladly helped whenever he was around. The swimming pool was something to behold. Joe had the pool designed in the shape of a left-handed boxing glove. Left-handed because Smokin' Joe's best punch was his left hook. It was Smokin' Joe's left hook that put Muhammad Ali on the canvas in the fifteenth round of their first fight in 1971. Ali survived the round after that punch, but most opponents hit by it, did not. The thumb of the boxing glove was a jacuzzi.

The two cousins, both quiet by nature, worked diligently at the pool cleaning. Marvis maneuvered the vacuum wand, while Bernard handled the skimmer. When there was talking, Marvis did most of it, Bernard responding with a shake of his head or a simple, "Uh, huh," to Marvis's occasional comment about his boxing training or his Cadillac Seville. The sound of the breezeway door shutting told Marvis that his sister Jacqui was home. From where he was standing, Marvis had a clear view to the breezeway walk through, but he had a, "Jacqui's home, so what," feeling and almost didn't even raise his head to

Chapter 11 A Storybook Romance ...

look at her. Then he did. It would be rather old fashioned to say that Marvis swooned at what he saw, but there is no better word to describe the reaction he had when he lifted his head and set his eyes on Daralyn Evon Lucas.

Daralyn Lucas was a new friend of Jacqui's, or at least one Marvis didn't know. Jacqui had a routine of bringing friends around to introduce to her big brother in hopes that he might like one of them and since they were almost always Christian girls, get Marvis "saved" in the process. "This is my unsaved brother, Marvis," was the way Jacqui usually started the introductions. So far, Marvis had not taken the bait with any of the girls Jacqui had brought over, but he had never seen the girl Jacqui had standing beside her now.

Although Daralyn was only fifteen, she had the looks of an adult. She had the figure and facial features of a model, with long wavy hair, warm smile, and beautiful dark eyes. Daralyn was stunningly beautiful, and Marvis was stunned. He stood like a statue staring at her. Except for the vacuum pole supporting him while he gawked and a, "Hey Lady," the scene could easily have been from a Jerry Lewis movie, with Marvis falling in the pool, clothes and all.

After Jacqui and her guest passed out of view and into the house, Marvis turned to his cousin Bernard, who had also been getting an eyeful. "Did you see that girl with Jacqui?" Marvis demanded of his cousin. Bernard was very reserved, but acknowledged what he knew Marvis was thinking. "She was a beauty alright," he answered. "Beauty? Beauty?" Marvis muttered, looking for some bigger way to express the chills he was feeling all over his body – or maybe some bolder way. "That's the girl I'm going to marry. She's going to be my wife!" Marvis declared as he turned off the vacuum pump and headed toward the house. Marvis was not a go getter when it came to girls. He was normally quiet and shy around them, but this was one girl friend of Jacqui's that Marvis wanted to meet. Bernard followed in silence, granting his approval with a humble nod of his head.

Before Marvis and Bernard made it to the house, they ran into Jacqui and Daralyn coming out. Jacqui started with, "This is my not-yet-saved brother."

Marvis interrupted her by blurting out in Daralyn's direction, "What's your name?"

Daralyn slowed the pace down by softly answering, "My name is Daralyn."

Marvis missed the cue to change the tempo by bursting forth with, "When can we go out?!"

Daralyn smiled and patiently responded, "Do you believe in God?"

To which Marvis answered, "Yeah, sure."

Daralyn added, "Have you made Christ the Lord of your life?"

Marvis, who was a bit flustered responded, "I ... believe in God."

Then came the kicker from Daralyn. "Well, the only way we can go out, is if you go to church with me."

(What?! I'm not going to church!) "Ohhhh, church, ahhh" (was this a scheme by his sister to drag him into church?), "well ... " (Maybe it can be like a trade off), "Okay!"

With that, the girls went back inside. Marvis began to follow, but Bernard nodded in the direction of the pool to remind his cousin that the cleaning wasn't finished. Marvis went back to the job, his head swimming with thoughts of "Daralyn" and their short first conversation. When the pool chores were finally done and all the equipment was put

Chapter 11   A Storybook Romance ...   149

away, the guys made a bee line for the house. Marvis had that nervous but excited feeling when he heard the voices of Jacqui and Daralyn in the game room in the cellar. He and Bernard went right on down. The room had a pool table, pin ball machine, and ping pong table, but the girls were just leaning against the furniture talking. Marvis took another nice long look at his sister's guest to be sure that his eyes had not been blinded by the light outside and that she really was as beautiful as he thought. Satisfied, though now unable to stop looking at her, Marvis tried to talk with Daralyn again. This time the words flowed much easier for him. He relaxed and the two had a pleasant conversation. Of course, the time passed much too quickly and suddenly, it seemed, Daralyn's ride home had arrived - but not before Marvis had managed to obtain both her phone number and permission to call. As she left, Marvis watched Daralyn go up the stairs and pass out of sight, still mesmerized by her beauty. Later that same night, Marvis called Daralyn for the first time.

Somehow, despite a schedule overloaded by boxing training, school work, and chores, Marvis found the time to call Daralyn every night from that day on. Their conversations covered all the usual topics for new couples their age as they tried to get to know each other better over the phone. But being two especially decent, respectful, young people, they always spoke to each other in a kind manner, never demanding, rude, or sarcastic. Marvis was also humbled by the image of such a beautiful woman on the other end of the line. Daralyn, too, possessed a great deal of humility, though she was not in awe of the fact that Marvis had a world famous father or that he was trying to follow in his father's footsteps, and she refused to back down on the condition for their dating.

"The only way we can go out, is if you go to church with me," were the words that had stuck in Marvis's craw that first day and a condition he hoped to get around with smooth talking on the phone as time passed. Marvis was a good kid, and he thought of himself as a Christian. After all, his mom and dad had taught him and his sisters right from wrong and, "a lot of stuff about God," plus, Mrs. Frazier made sure they all went to Sunday School every week. Marvis believed what he had been taught about religion, but he didn't take it as far as his oldest sister did. Jacqui was always talking about Jesus and "being saved." "Where are you going to spend eternity?" she would often ask him when she got going on religion. Eternity? Marvis was a lot more concerned about getting all the chores for the week done before Pop got home. And yet, there Marvis was on the first Sunday after he and Daralyn met, sitting in her church, listening to Pastor Obe Clark preach about the need to have Jesus Christ come into your life as your personal Lord and Savior.

Pastor Clark was a strong preacher and a sincere seeker who, when he spoke, in and out of the pulpit, was sure of his convictions and dutiful to his purpose - leading people to the Lord. His deep voice and direct look added an intensity to the words that he spoke so fluently. Drawn by an infatuation for Daralyn that was rapidly becoming genuine affection, Marvis was largely immune to the words of the pastor as he attended services with Daralyn week after week, services which if he missed meant missing seeing her at all. However, undetected by Marvis, the words of Obe Clark were getting in, the prayers of Jacqui were being heard, the spirit of the Lord was moving, and Marvis's "divine appointment" was fast approaching. The seventh Sunday of services that he attended with Daralyn would be the beginning of a new life for Marvis Frazier.

Almost two months after they first met, contact between Marvis and Daralyn was still restricted to church services and nightly phone calls. By this time, however, Marvis had gotten his driver's license and was allowed to drive Daralyn to church in his new Cadillac Seville. Like he did the previous six Sundays, Marvis spent most of the service delighting in the time spent in Daralyn's presence, speaking to her softly in person, looking at her beauty in detail, and holding her hand. Though Marvis stood at the appropriate times, sang along with the hymns, and closed his eyes during prayer; he really wasn't paying much attention to anything, except Daralyn. It was from this enchanted state that Marvis suddenly became aware of Pastor Clark's voice during the altar call at the end of that seventh Sunday service.

"You've been coming to this church week after week and month after month," Pastor Clark's voice belted out, "God wants to use you. He has a plan for you."

Marvis looked up toward the altar at the front of the church, where other guests were already going forward in response to the Pastor's call to those who needed salvation. The pastor seemed to be looking right at him. "Why is this guy talking to me like that?" Marvis thought, "He's talking right to me."

Pastor Clark continued, pronouncing each word slowly and with authority, "What if you die today? If you do not have Christ in your life, do you know where you are going? The bible says in Romans 6:23 that 'the wages of sin is death, but the gift of God is eternal life through Jesus Christ our Lord.'"

Marvis's heart was beating faster and faster.

"God is trying to call YOU. He wants to use YOU."

"Man, this guy's talking right to me!" Marvis said to himself. "I know it's me ... use me for what? Why doesn't he stop?"

Just then, a girl about his age, who was sitting directly in front of him but three pews closer to the front, got up and started to go forward.

"Whew," Marvis thought, "that was close ... he was talking about that girl." His heart was still racing from the close call.

"Praise the Lord for this young soul," Pastor Clark exclaimed upon seeing the teenager rise from her seat, "but No! No! God is not done here today. YOU have been coming to this church week after week and month after month. God wants to use YOU. He has a plan for YOU."

"Me? God has a plan for me?" Marvis was sweating. Marvis was shaking. He had never felt this way before. He was feeling the power of conviction. "Oh no, not me ... but I'm sure he means me. The guy is looking right at me."

Pastor Clark raised his arms and peered heavenward, but when he looked down again his eyes seemed to fall right on Marvis, and his hands seemed to reach right out to touch him. "God wants YOU to be a tool for Him (Marvis). God wants YOU to spread the news of what He can do and how He can change lives (Marvis)."

It was useless to fight it. There was nothing Marvis could do now, except obey the Holy Spirit. He stood. Daralyn gave his hand a gentle squeeze. Nervous, but relieved, Marvis turned and started for the altar. These were his first steps in a new life of accepting and serving Jesus Christ as his personal Lord and Savior. At the altar, Marvis knelt in prayer and was saved.

There was cause for celebration at Obe Clark's church that day - several people had been born again. Parishioner

Chapter 11   A Storybook Romance ...

Daralyn Evon Lucas had special cause for her happiness. Marvis Frazier, the young man whom she was becoming quite fond of, had become a Christian. Now she could let her feelings for him develop further. Now she could talk with him openly about the future. And now, since Marvis was saved, they could finally start to date.

*   *   *

Still years before they were married and only months after they had met, Marvis and Daralyn began to think of their relationship as "God ordained." Daralyn was elated that Marvis had become a Christian. Marvis was enthralled by Daralyn, thinking, "How did I get so lucky?" They shared a kind of romance that was almost to good to be true, but it was. Two decent young people who were immune to the vices that affected most kids their age. Neither one partied, smoked, drank, nor even cursed. They each loved their families, respected their parents, and took their responsibilities seriously, Marvis his boxing and chores, Daralyn her school work and religious training. When they came together, a circle formed around the couple that kept the world out and made it easier for them to be different, to be good in the face of so much that wasn't.

Surprisingly, Marvis and Daralyn didn't really spend much time together. They lived in different neighborhoods and went to different schools, and Marvis was beginning to travel a lot with his amateur boxing. They did, however, continue the nightly phone calls and church services on Sundays. Occasionally they found time to go out on a date, maybe to a movie or a Bible study. Still, their affection for each other grew stronger and stronger until at some point it became love. Many of Daralyn's friends and family called her Day, but Marvis called her his Lady Day. Not long after they met, Marvis started telling his "Lady Day" that he wanted to marry her. Daralyn, the more sensible of the two, would say, "You're crazy." Marvis would reply, "Yeah, about you."

Whether Marvis's matrimonial desires were serious at such a young age or not, Daralyn's levelheadedness prevailed, and it would be seven long years before the two tied the knot. During that time, the routine events of adolescence guided them each into adulthood. Marvis attended Plymouth-Whitemarsh High School, where he had two more years. Daralyn had three years left at the Christian Academy she attended. Marvis enjoyed high school but placed more importance on his boxing career. Daralyn was a good student who wanted to enter the teaching profession, so she was more focused on her studies.

When Marvis finished high school, he jumped into boxing full time. Although still an amateur, his success justified the time and energy he was putting into the sport. An excellent amateur career was already assured, his prospects for the Olympics were bright, and eventual professional status was realistic. Daralyn loved Marvis but never really liked boxing. She supported his choice to be a boxer though, and showed that support by attending many of his matches, amateur and professional. Marvis was not bothered by Daralyn's lack of interest in the sport. Instead he actually preferred that Daralyn stay in the background, where she would be shielded from the hurtful things that can happen when one is in the limelight.

Upon finishing high school, Daralyn entered Howard University in Washington, D.C. While Marvis was immersed in his amateur boxing career, Daralyn began the studies necessary for a degree in elementary education. The separation of the two was hard on them both. Although Washington to Philadelphia was only a few hours by car, Marvis often traveled throughout the United States (and sometimes worldwide) for his matches. The situation left little opportunity for them to be together. The nightly phone calls came to the rescue day after day, and occasional letters helped soothe the aching hearts. Marvis wanted them to go ahead and marry sooner than planned, but Daralyn said no, insisting that she finish college and they have enough money for a house.

By the time Daralyn completed college, Marvis had already turned professional and was saving for the house. His career as a professional mirrored his early amateur days. He was undefeated and gaining momentum with every fight. With her studies over and his traveling reduced, the two were finally back together, this time for good. Their relationship was like a fairy tale. It was just as they had imagined it. Marvis and Daralyn were very happy as they began making plans for their wedding.

It would be a July wedding in 1983. Marvis's best friend, Andrew, would be his best man, and Daralyn's high school friend would be the maid of honor. It would be a big affair, too big for their home church, so it was moved to Greater Harvest Church which was also in Philadelphia. In order to provide space for all of the friends and family who attended, the reception was held at the Frazier's home. Though Daralyn's father had unfortunately passed away not long before the wedding, Poppa Joe pronounced his blessing on the union when he told Marvis, "You did fine with this one, Son." It was a dream come true wedding followed by a dream come true honeymoon. Marvis and Daralyn spent their first week alone together as man and wife on a cruise ship in the Caribbean. The only interruption was a brief phone call from Smokin' Joe, asking Marvis if he would like to fight Larry Holmes for the heavyweight championship of the world. Little did Marvis and Daralyn realize then that the effects of that call would cast a shadow over their lives for more than five years.

When Marvis and Daralyn returned from their honeymoon, Marvis had four months to prepare for his fight with Larry Holmes. This was the fight of his dreams, a fight for the heavyweight championship of the world – his opportunity to return the title to the Frazier family and become the first father/son heavyweight champions. Marvis prepared in earnest. Daralyn, meanwhile, turned her attention to job openings for elementary school teachers. She had performed well in college and was an excellent candidate, but before she could find placement, Daralyn discovered that she was pregnant and temporarily abandoned her search. Marvis had set aside plenty of money for a down payment on a house, but because Daralyn's mom was living alone, the newlyweds decided to move in with her for the time being to give her company and to make things easier for everyone. Even with the thrill of the "big" fight with Holmes, the excitement of a new baby coming, and all the work to get ready for both, Marvis and Daralyn were the model of a happy couple. After years of anticipated bliss, often only sustained by phone calls and letters, the two were finally together as husband and wife, playing the roles they had imagined and enjoying every minute of it.

Six months before the November 25th, 1983, fight against twenty-three year old Marvis Frazier, Larry Holmes had narrowly squeezed by a tough young boxer named

Tim Witherspoon with a controversial twelve round split decision. Marvis Frazier had beaten Tim Witherspoon as an amateur. Going into his fight with Holmes, Marvis was undefeated in ten fights and flying high with impressive wins against James Broad and Joe Bugner in his previous two outings. Unfortunately for Marvis, despite missing with over fifty jabs in the first two minutes of their fight, Larry Holmes found his target with an explosive overhand right and put Marvis on the canvas with just under a minute to go in the first round. Marvis quickly recovered, but Holmes pinned him in the corner and bombed away until the referee stopped the fight with only three seconds to go in the round. At that moment Marvis Frazier's dreams were shattered, and Marvis was crushed.

Daralyn watched the fight in misery for her husband and expected him to be emotionally distraught over the loss, but she had no idea of the depth of the hole he had fallen into and the depression that would follow. The week following the fight was spent in California trying to help Marvis snap out of his doldrums, but to no avail. Upon their return to Philadelphia, Daralyn was surprised to see Marvis avoid returning to the gym. Still, she felt it was only a matter of time before he would be his old, joyful, happy go lucky self again. After months of moodiness and his continued avoidance of the gym, Daralyn's concerns for her husband's condition were validated when he opened up to his wife with the simple question, "What is wrong with me?"

Marvis's depression would last five years and encompass the entire balance of his boxing career. It was diagnosed as clinical depression about two years after it started. Marvis tried psychotherapy and drug therapy briefly without satisfactory results, though eventually turning to his religious faith helped him with decisions that brought relief. Daralyn was very patient and supportive of Marvis throughout his ordeal, despite its adverse affect on their marriage. It bothered her that she did not have an answer for him when he asked over and over, "What is wrong with me?" Sometimes it wore on her nerves, prompting the usually soft spoken woman to once respond, "I don't know Marvis. I'm not God!"

In the meantime, they did have a marriage to attend to and the young couple did their best to cope. Daralyn gave birth to their first child, Tamyra, in 1984. The new parents hoped that this baby girl would help rid Marvis of the blues, which it did to some extent but not completely and only temporarily. By the summer of that same year, the couple found a nice house in Wyncote and moved in to set up their own home. When baby Tamyra was old enough for day care, Daralyn finally found that teaching job. Not long after, Marvis returned to the gym and began to put his boxing career back together. By September of 1984 he was fighting (and winning) again.

Still, there would be four more years of depression to deal with. During those four years, Daralyn would give birth to their second child, Tiara, born in March of 1986. That event led to one of the few disagreements Marvis and Daralyn ever had. Marvis always wanted to have a lot of children, maybe eleven or twelve. Daralyn only wanted two.

"When we get married, let's have a lot of kids."

"NO, Marvis, ONLY TWO." And they left it at that, until Tiara was born - the second girl in two tries.

Marvis loved his two beautiful daughters, nevertheless, "We gotta try one more time; we gotta get the boy!"

To which Daralyn responded, "NO, I gave you

two chances Marvis and that's it!" Proof that although Daralyn was very soft spoken, if you crossed her, you would hear from her about it.

After his loss to Mike Tyson in July of 1986, when it seemed that Marvis's depression was deeper than ever and there was no relief in sight, Marvis started to make changes in his life that allowed a bit of light to shine at the end of the tunnel. It was as though he had to be beaten so convincingly in the ring, that he would not look to boxing again as an avenue to success and an end to his depression. Once he had that change of thinking, he looked to God for the cure to his depression and seriously considered retirement from the sport that had been the main focus in his life since he was sixteen years old. It was a freeing feeling, scary to be sure, but exhilarating.

Cautiously and keeping it to himself, Marvis began to ponder an existence outside of boxing. At the same time, he started to turn his life increasingly over to the service of God, including spending more time with his family in an attempt to be a better father. While these subtle changes were being made, Marvis continued to go to the gym, but less frequently and sometimes to help out with the other boxers more than to work out himself. In the course of the next two years, Marvis only fought three times. The first two fights were to assure himself that he wasn't completely washed up after the loss to "Iron" Mike, and the third to be sure that his thoughts of retirement were not misplaced. He won all three of these fights, but winning or losing wasn't as important as how he felt about them. The results were as he expected. His heart was no longer in the ring and God's plan for his life was elsewhere.

Not long after his final fight in October, 1988, Marvis

surprised Daralyn at breakfast with the announcement that he was retiring from boxing. "Okay," was Daralyn's simple response. She was pleased but not fully aware of how much this decision would be a blessing to their family and a renewal of the love between them.

> *"When you cry out, 'Why is this happening to me, God? I'm trying to live according to Your Word,' you have to remember that sometimes suffering here on earth, even when you are trying to do the will of God, can be God letting the devil succeed in order to test the strength of your faith in Him, just like what happened to Job in the Old Testament. Will you curse God when bad things happen to you, or will you stand firm in your faith and remember God's promises?"*
> *(Marvis Frazier in a 2012 interview answering a question about the losses he experienced in his life.)*

Marvis and Daralyn tie the knot. Best man Andrew is visible over Marvis's right shoulder. (Photo courtesy of Darryl Lee)

Chapter 12

... with a Sad Ending

"God, please don't take my Lady Day away."

During the five years following Marvis Frazier's retirement, while Larry Holmes was making an incredible comeback and Mike Tyson was losing the title to James "Buster" Douglas in the greatest upset in boxing history, Marvis was re-establishing his life around his Lord and his family. Boxing was still an important part of his life. He was a fixture at his dad's gym, helping with the training of the young fighters, but his heart and soul were drawn more toward service to Christ and striving to be a better father to his girls and husband to his wife.

The relationship between Daralyn and Marvis had always been good in that each cared for the well being of the other, but when retirement from boxing also relieved Marvis of his depression, it was as though a cloud was lifted and joyful sunshine flooded in to refill their marriage with happiness.

Being retired from boxing did not change the structure of Marvis's family life much. After all, he continued to work at his father's gym whenever possible, expanded his involvement with Prison Fellowship to the point of a full time occupation, and began to answer a calling to minister in Faith Temple, the small church the family attended. Daralyn, meanwhile, was teaching elementary school full time, while the children, Tamyra and Tiara, were finally in school themselves as young students. It was, before and after Marvis's retirement, a very busy family.

However, it was the mood that had changed. With his retirement from boxing the weight of depression had been lifted from Marvis and he was again the funny, lighthearted man he had once been. He was fun to be with and thoughtful of others, especially his family. Marvis engaged his young daughters in rollicking play, not unlike his father had done with Marvis and his sisters. The Frazier home in Wyncote was now filled with unrestricted giggling and joyful shrieks from the girls and jubilant laughter from Dad. With Daralyn, Marvis was again the compassionate partner in marriage who indulged her with affection. No longer did she have to deal with his nearly daily plea of, "What is wrong with me?" and all that question implied. Instead, Marvis was again the man of the house, who bounded in from a day at the gym or returned home from a trip, to shower Daralyn with hugs, kisses, compliments, and sometimes flowers or gifts.

As the years passed, Marvis continued to care for his family the best he could considering he was a man engaged in two very time consuming occupations (work at the gym and traveling with Prison Fellowship), with a third job hovering in the wings (his upcoming work as a preacher and evangelist). Despite time constraints and the stress from his constant need to rush from one responsibility to the next, Marvis always made it a priority to help Daralyn with family events. He enjoyed his time spent celebrating birthdays, putting together gift baskets for easter, helping to prepare for the Thanksgiving gathering, and decorating for Christmas. But it wasn't just with holidays that Marvis tried to put the family first. When his oldest daughter Tamyra showed an interest in basketball an excited Marvis was there to cheer her on. In keeping with his jovial personality, Marvis often whooped it up at those games, jokingly calling out individual players by name or number, singing songs, and leading cheers among the hometown fans. While Marvis watched his daughter's contests, he might occasionally think about his own school sports activities, which included basketball (along with football, baseball, and wrestling), but he rarely thought about his past career as a boxer and never looked back on it with regret. He was too busy enjoying the new life that had replaced it.

Eventually, the huge demands of his work schedule did impinge on his time with Daralyn and the girls. Marvis continued to work at the gym when he was available, but by the mid 1990's the work of God was taking the biggest share of his time, especially when a few years earlier Marvis began to answer the calling he felt to the pastorate and evangelism.

In order to become a minister in the Faith Temple Church of God, Marvis had to start as an usher. As an usher he greeted parishioners, distributed bulletins and programs, and collected tithes and offerings. After Marvis had served for over a year he applied to become a deacon, a lay person who assists the pastor in various functions. While in this position, Marvis received informal training by the pastor as well as began his formal training for the ministry.

After more than three years of serving as a deacon and studying under Faith Temple pastor Fulton, the pastor felt that Marvis was ready to be ordained. In the fall of 1994, with his wife and daughters proudly looking on and his father, Joe, and his mother, Florence, in attendance, Marvis performed his first service. As a minister, Marvis was occasionally called on to preach to the congregation at Faith Temple, but he was frequently asked to speak at other churches' evangelical events, where he became quite adept at combining his boxing experiences and stories about his father with the message of salvation.

In the meantime, his work with Prison Fellowship was increasing. As the 1990's flew by and the new millenium approached, Marvis found himself on the road nearly full time in his capacity as an athlete/celebrity selected by the Prison Fellowship organization to witness and minister to prisoners throughout the United States. It was during one of these Prison Fellowship road trips that Marvis received the most disturbing phone call of his life.

Late in the spring of 2001, Marvis was traveling with Prison Fellowship throughout warm, sunny Florida. The weather back home in Philadelphia was cold and wet. Usually Marvis called Daralyn each evening after work, but on this particular evening Daralyn called him before he had a chance. The call was routine at first with Marvis asking about the girls then launching into a story about some touching or funny thing that happened en route to the facility his group was ministering at that day. Part way through his story, Daralyn cut him off. "Marvis, I have cancer."

"What?"

Daralyn continued, "You know that I haven't been feeling good for a couple of weeks now ... "

"Yes, but that was just the flu or something. You look fine..."

"You remember Marvis, I got some tests last week."

Marvis weakly interrupted, "But baby ... "

Daralyn persisted, "I went to see my doctor today. The tests were back. I have cancer."

Marvis was floored by her words but hid his shock while he responded. "Well, the Lord will take care of you. You don't have to worry about that. We'll be alright."

"It's colon cancer, Daralyn said with little change in her voice, "and they think it's in my liver. The cancer has already spread." With that, Daralyn was unable to hold back her emotions any longer.

Marvis also broke down when he heard Daralyn's sobs. Even through his tears, Marvis tried to console his wife. "I'm coming right home. I'm gonna get a plane and I'll be home tonight. We'll be alright."

Marvis hung up the phone and turned to his friends and co-workers in the Prison Fellowship group. They could tell something wasn't right by the look on his face. As they moved closer and formed a half circle around him, Marvis tearfully told them about the conversation with Daralyn. Everyone encouraged him to go right home. He should be with his wife, and they would pick up the slack. "Don't worry," he was told, "We're all praying for you."

On his way home that night, Marvis was full of thought. He knew that cancer ran in Daralyn's family. Her father had died of cancer just before Marvis and Daralyn were married, and her older sister, Collette, had survived cancer. Even so, Marvis never feared that cancer would affect Daralyn, because she and Marvis were good people doing the work of the Lord. Why then had she become afflicted? Was this a test of their faith? Maybe God was going to use Daralyn to demonstrate His healing power. Marvis lowered his head right there in the plane and prayed quietly to himself. "Lord, I know You are not going to take my wife. I know You are not going to take her because we are doing Your will. We are living right and doing what You want us to do. Please don't take my wife."

After two short flights, with a long layover in North Carolina, Marvis arrived home in the middle of the night. Daralyn was already asleep. The former heavyweight contender slipped quietly into bed beside his childhood sweetheart, cradling her gently in his arms until morning.

The next day, Marvis and Daralyn discussed the situation in more detail. Daralyn, who looked perfectly healthy to Marvis, cried as she explained to Marvis that her doctor didn't think that there was anything that could be done. Marvis couldn't believe what he was hearing and blurted out, "Man, we've got to go some place else!" To Marvis the some place else was simple. Whenever Marvis needed hospitalization during his boxing career, he had gone to Pennsylvania Hospital. It was at Pennsylvania Hospital that Marvis had had his neck surgery. Marvis reasoned that since, "They were the ones who fixed me, they can fix Daralyn." By the end of the day, arrangements had been made for Marvis and Daralyn to go see a specialist at Pennsylvania Hospital. The appointment was set for later in the week so that the oncologist would have time to receive and review the test results.

The doctor was different, but the prognosis was the same. "I'm sorry Mr. Frazier ... she's really bad ... it's terminal."

Marvis jumped up from his seat. "NO!" he thought, wanting to slam his fist on the doctor's desk, but instead keeping his cool and smiling confidently while he announced, "Lady, you don't know what you are talking about. We've got God on our side!"

Still, the doctor went on with her professional duty, informing the couple that while Daralyn looked fine on the outside, the cancer cells had already spread in her body; and since it was so advanced, there was no treatment available that could stop it. Finally the doctor laid it all out on the table, finishing with, "Daralyn probably has less than six months to live."

In their eighteen year marriage, Daralyn had always been a wife who took care of her man, especially when he was busy boxing or deep in depression. Now Marvis would be taking care of her. For a few weeks after hearing the prognosis of the doctors, Daralyn, although not feeling well, was able to carry on her routines at home. Marvis used this time to get their house in order. He contacted everyone who he felt should know about their predicament, and he made arrangements for a leave of absence with the Prison Fellowship organization. Marvis also counseled with his pastor at church to help set in motion whatever would be needed, spiritually, for Daralyn's healing through the power of God.

Marvis and Daralyn accepted that there was nothing more the medical profession could do for her, but they did not accept the notion that Daralyn could not be healed. "The Lord will take care of you. You don't have to worry about that. We'll be alright. We've got God on our side."

Daralyn's daughters, Tamyra and Tiara, now seventeen and fifteen agreed with their father. "You are going to make it," they would tell their mother. "God will deliver you from this disease."

Eventually, despite the strong faith of her whole family, the cancer spread throughout Daralyn's body and her condition worsened. Daralyn lost the strength in her legs and could no longer walk. By that time, Marvis was her full time caretaker. He provided a wheel chair so that Daralyn could move throughout the house, and when the late summer weather was nice, Marvis would take her out and wheel her around outside. Their house was in a pleasant development off the main thoroughfare. The streets in their neighborhood were lined with large, beautiful trees. While pushing her around the block, Marvis would reassure his wife that she was going to make it, and that the Lord would take care of her.

Soon, more than her legs were weakened, and even the wheel chair had to be abandoned. Daralyn was forced to stay in bed. Yet, Marvis and Daralyn would not give up the faith that she would be released from the grip of this disease. Once, while Daralyn could still speak, Marvis was praying with her when she suddenly cried out, "How long, Lord? "How long are you going to let me be like this?" Was it freedom from the cancer she wanted or freedom from the struggle against it? Was she looking back to health on this earth or looking forward to being with Jesus in heaven?

After that day, the end came very quickly. Daralyn soon lost her ability to speak or respond to Marvis in any way. "I know you can hear me. We're still fighting all the way through, Baby. We're gonna make it," he would tell her over and over as he sat by her side, gently squeezing her hand just as she had squeezed his on the day of his salvation so many years before. The family had complete trust that God would take care of Daralyn, yet at some point, Marvis and the girls asked Hospice to be present to administer medication to help Daralyn be more comfortable in case she was in pain.

Then one day in November, 2001, it was over. Marvis remembers that, "She closed her eyes and God just took her." Realizing that Daralyn had died, Marvis was numb. He felt lost. He cried as he kneeled by her side and prayed, "Lord, I don't know why, but You took her for a reason." Her funeral was standing room only – the whole church was packed. Despite dying of a disease that had ravaged her body, Marvis thought that his darling Daralyn looked beautiful.

In a 2012 interview about his wife having cancer, Marvis responded to a question about Daralyn's condition in the following way.
<u>*Jamie:*</u> *What did the specialist at Pennsylvania Hospital say when you and Daralyn went to see her?*
<u>*Marvis:*</u> *"She said," (he struggled to answer) "I'm ... I'm, I'm sorry, Mr. Frazier," (he paused, then stuttered) "she's, she, she, she, she, she, she's really bad ...,"(then he spoke quietly) "it's terminal ...," (Marvis paused again before continuing) "I'm sorry, Mr. Frazier."*

Part IV Changes

Some changes look negative on the surface but you will soon realize that space is being created in your life for something new to emerge.
- Eckhart Tolle

*Marvis and daughters Tamyra and Tiara.
(Photo courtesy of Darryl Lee)*

Chapter 13

Life Without Daralyn

"Why would You take my girls' mom? I don't understand why You allowed her to go, because they need a mom. I'm just a dad. I don't know anything about being a mom."

At the time of Daralyn's death in 2001, Marvis was forty-one years old. The two had met in 1976 when Marvis was only sixteen. He and Daralyn had been together over half of his life and all of his adult life. The loss of Daralyn was desolating to Marvis. All of the disappointments and setbacks in his life rolled into one were like a drop in the ocean compared to the empty feeling he had in his heart from her passing. His paralysis in the Olympic trials was like fate saying no contest, his defeat by Larry Holmes was like a disqualification, his thrashing by Mike Tyson was a mere slip on the canvas, his bout with depression was just a low blow, but the loss of his soul mate was a down for the count knockout. It was the punch Marvis didn't see coming, the punch, he says, that always gets you. Being a fighter, Marvis got up off the canvas soon after he was counted out, but the pain of that fall would stay with him for years.

Marvis, like most people who suffer the loss of a spouse, gravitated toward the closest connection to his wife. Responding to the needs of Tamyra and Tiara, while at the same time (but less consciously) taking care of his own, Marvis rallied around his two daughters. Tamyra, who was nearly eighteen, was a star basketball player and already attending college. Tiara, who trailed Tamyra by two years, was still in high school. Marvis wanted to do his best to provide the parenting the girls needed as they approached adulthood, especially now that they were suffering the loss of their mom. He knew he couldn't replace the mothering Daralyn gave the girls, but he hoped to at least continue to be a good father and try to help them understand Daralyn's death. The explanation that Marvis shared with Tamyra and Tiara was the same one that he embraced to answer his own question of why God took their mother. For that answer Marvis focused on the story of Job in the Old Testament. In the Book of Job, we read of a righteous man who fears God and shuns evil. God declares His servant blameless and upright, but Satan questions Job's character, claiming that his love of God is conditional on the many blessings God has bestowed upon him. Take them away and Job will surely turn his back on the one he calls his Redeemer. Satan is allowed by God to cause Job great losses, tempting Job to curse God, but Job refuses to do so, setting the example of how believers should react to trials and tribulations in life. Christians should continue to love God unconditionally, even while suffering for reasons they don't understand. Marvis shared this belief with his daughters, explaining that the devil always has a hand in the workings of this world. So, when bad things happen to you, even as severe as the loss of a loved one, you should stand firm in your faith and remember God's promises.

    Marvis made a steadfast effort to convince his daughters of the Christian tenet of perseverance in the face of great suffering, yet how could he ever convince himself? How could Marvis accept Daralyn's death when it was such a harsh blow and so disruptive to his family? Still, if Marvis ever entertained any doubts or if his faith ever faltered, he never showed it. Marvis never claimed to know the reason God took Daralyn from them ("maybe God needed another beautiful voice for His heavenly choir"), but like Job, Marvis held firm to his belief that his Redeemer lives and everything is happening according to His plan. Marvis was comfortable in his convictions, and this helped him to begin moving forward. However, before the pain of that loss was soothed sufficiently by time, Marvis was tested again.

Less than two years after his wife had died of cancer, Marvis received the shocking news that his oldest daughter, Tamyra, was diagnosed with the same dreaded disease. Not yet twenty years old and just one week into resuming her college studies, Tamyra was found to have non-Hodgkin's lymphoma, a form of cancer of the lymph system which can result in death if it fails to respond to chemotherapy.

Though he kept it to himself, Marvis was stunned and in a state of near disbelief. It seemed as though he was living in a bad dream. Nevertheless, for the sake of Tamyra, Marvis mobilized his seemingly unwavering faith and began to pray and affirm with his voice that his daughter would be victorious over the disease. Tamyra underwent eight chemotherapy treatments, and the cancer went into remission. Marvis praised God and breathed a sigh of relief.

Although Marvis's faith in God survived and, in a way, thrived during the trials and tribulations his family experienced with cancer, on an operating level his religious practices did suffer. All three of his religious activities were altered in response to the requirements of being a single parent. The most significant change was the decision by Marvis to retire from Prison Fellowship. Marvis loved that ministry and was well suited to it. Still, Marvis felt that he could not continue being on the road, away from the girls, without Daralyn being there for them. In the meantime, the Prison Fellowship organization was going through some changes of its own, having recently selected a new chief executive officer. The result was fewer opportunities for Marvis to go on the road for them, so, it was the ideal time for him to make the change. Similarly, Marvis decided to cut back on his preaching and evangelizing. That was an important activity to Marvis, but with his other responsibilities, even before Daralyn became ill, he was not able to spend the preparation and follow up time he really felt was necessary to properly perform those religious duties. Of course, now that he was trying to be both mother and father to his girls, Marvis was even less able to do the job the way he thought it should be done. The final change concerned Faith Temple Church of God. Marvis found it difficult to attend the same church, without Daralyn, that they had attended together for seventeen years. He decided a change in churches would be helpful. Not far from his home in Wyncote was the church his daughters were already attending. Enon Tabernacle Baptist Church welcomed Marvis Frazier with open arms.

Working at his dad's gym was the one activity that Marvis did not cut back on. As a matter of fact, no longer being on the road with Prison Fellowship and preaching less, along with attending a church closer to home, Marvis actually had more time to spend at Joe Frazier's Gym than ever. It made him feel good. Being there made him feel warm and comfortable. Later, when Tamyra and Tiara were both out of the house and on their own, Marvis could be found at the gym most of the time. Why go back home to an empty house? There was plenty that needed to be done at the gym. Marvis began going in early and staying

Chapter 13   Life Without Daralyn   177

late nearly every day.

As a young boxer in training twenty years earlier, with his vision constricted by the blinders of youth, Marvis had been guilty of seeing the gym as little more than a place to box. Sure, he respected the fact that his father, the great Smokin' Joe Frazier, owned it and that a parade of talented pugilists, established and otherwise, had come through the doors to test, perfect, and prove their skills, but it wasn't until he began to interact with Joe Frazier's Gym with much more on his mind than becoming the next heavyweight champion of the world that Marvis began to recognize its potential.

The changes started with Joe, who, approaching age sixty and struggling with injuries from an automobile accident, was tiring of running the gym. After he unsuccessfully tried to hire an outsider to take over its management, Joe turned to Marvis with "Well, you gonna run it, Son."

Without a moment's hesitation, Marvis responded, "I can do it."

Typically, a father who is passing the reins to a son can have trouble letting go, causing problems for both. Not so with Joe. It was still "Joe Frazier's Gym," but Joe knew Marvis was a good man, who would do things the way they were supposed to be done. Marvis did not let his father down. Without college training in business, accounting, or marketing, Marvis was performing all of these functions capably. Additionally, he was training fighters and helping Joe with personal appearances and endorsements. Marvis's business theory was simple, "As long as you do things right, things end up right." Nobody was getting rich, but all the bills were being paid.

By the mid 2000's, the gym had come to mean much more to Marvis than he ever expected it to. He realized that the gym was now the driving force in his life. The operation of this old landmark had become the vehicle for those things he was most passionate about, teaching boxing and training boxers, working with people, witnessing for Christ, helping needy kids, and impacting his community in a positive way. The gym was an interface with the surrounding neighborhood, through which Marvis and his staff could reach out to people of all ages and all walks of life. With the one golden rule of "love and keep on loving," Marvis and crew were touching lives and transforming people. Years after her death, Marvis still missed Daralyn, but he was moving on and the gym was helping him to do so.

"It's about giving back ... trying to make a difference in the community, trying to touch young men and women ... If we don't reach out and touch people, who is going to do it? So what we try to do is show leadership ... and we try to show love." (Marvis talking about the work of the gym in the 2008 documentary Thrilla in Manila.)

(Photo courtesy of Webster Riddick)

Chapter 14

A New Dream

"The Lord giveth and the Lord taketh away" (A popular paraphrase of the Old Testament book of Job, Chapter 1, (part of) verse 21)

One fall day in 2005, while stuck in traffic, Marvis noticed all the renovations that were underway in North Philadelphia. In particular he liked the changes being made at Temple University, which was located less than a mile from the gym on North Broad Street. Everything looked so new, fresh, and active. The recent construction seemed to energize the area. As he drove through the bottleneck and continued to his destination, Marvis found himself thinking about the condition of his dad's gym. Why couldn't the gym be renovated? Wouldn't it be wonderful to energize their part of North Broad Street too, starting with some reconstruction at Joe Frazier's Gym?

That night, lying in bed, Marvis thought more seriously about the condition of the gym. At first he focused on things that had fallen into disrepair and needed work, like the roof, which had started to leak here and there during heavy rains, and some of the carpets that needed to be replaced. Details of upkeep were always on his mind, and maintenance of an old building like the one that housed his dad's gym took a steady flow of money. At times the regular bills just had to take priority while repairs fell behind. However, as he was falling asleep that night, Marvis let his mind wander from these stressful thoughts. Instead, he imagined that funding was not a concern and that the gym could be remodeled any way he wished. "Just imagine," he thought (as though he was talking to his dad), "we could do so much with all the space our building has. All four floors could be put to use ... there's so much room ... better training facilities ... a workout room ... for the community ... all ages ..." ....finally sleep overtook him.

A few days later, while enjoying the early morning sun, Marvis was cleaning up outside the gym before going inside to open for the day. As Marvis stooped to pick up some broken glass from the sidewalk, two people in business suits approached him from the parking area. Marvis noticed them right away, yet he didn't recall seeing the visitors walking up North Broad Street or a car pulling into the gym parking lot. Marvis doesn't remember what they said to him when they reached out to shake hands, only that they were very friendly and he felt completely at ease in their presence. At the time, Marvis suspected his guests were salespeople of some sort and, indeed, they began to talk to him about the gym operations and advertising. Just the same, when Marvis talks about his visitors now, he refers to them as the angels who came to perform a miracle. As the conversation became more of a sales presentation, Marvis politely responded with nods of his head at the appropriate times. He assumed they would be finished soon; he would thank them, take their business card, and they would be on their way.

Marvis seemed to be correct in his assessment of the situation. The salespeople wrapped up their talk, took turns re-shaking his hand, then started to walk away. Marvis went back to picking up broken glass; then he heard the question. One of the visitors had turned around. "Marvis," he said as though they were old friends, "do you have a dream for the gym?" To Marvis, the term "dream" had a special place in his life. Marvis was a man driven by dreams. He had dreamed of winning an Olympic Gold Medal. He had dreamed of becoming the heavyweight champion of the world.

Marvis straightened up and walked toward the visitors. "Why yes. Yes, I do have a dream for the gym ... C'mon inside ... I'd like to share it with you."

Now that Marvis had engaged his "angels" (or had they engaged him?), the "miracle" really began to unfold. Once inside the gym the three talked at length about his dream of renovating the building and somehow incorporating space for a community center with counseling services, workout rooms with physical therapy equipment, better boxing facilities – maybe even a museum. The talk session was capped off with a tour of the building during which Marvis unabashedly showed them all the available spaces to work with, despite the run down condition of much of the building.

Hours later, as Marvis walked them to the door, he felt his excitement diminish. Maybe laying everything out for them the way he had was too much, and he would never see his visitors again. "Don't worry Marvis. We'll get back to you," they told him almost in unison, as they slipped out the door.

Although Marvis did not really expect anything more to come from that encounter, he felt good about the exchange. That was the first time he had shared his thoughts about having the gym renovated, and possibly, if nothing else, he had planted some seeds. Marvis believed that a person never knows when and where the "seeds" they plant will sprout and grow, so he always tried to plant only good "seeds" in his dealings with others. All the same, Marvis went on with his daily work routines at the gym as though nothing had happened. One week passed without much thought of the salespeople he had met. A second week passed, and Marvis had almost forgotten the whole thing. Then, sometime during the third week, there was a call for Marvis in the office. The call was from an advertising agency.

"Marvis, I have something I want to show you. I think you are really going to like it." the voice on the other end of the line stated. "Can we get together today or tomorrow?"

Later that day, in the upstairs office of the gym, one of the "angels" laid out the plans for a "miracle." The package he presented to Marvis was entitled "Vision of the Future (a unique advertising opportunity)" and included a detailed description of a project to be known as "The Frazier Center," defined as, "a complete renovation inside and out of the property housing Joe Frazier's Gym." The plans included refurbishing the original boxing gym and adding a full fitness gym and physical therapy center, a community center with services for all ages including life counseling and educational training programs, and a world class boxing museum. The extensive plans also included food services, a pro shop, renovated office space, and the entire fourth floor dedicated to a Frazier family residence. A mission statement page provided the purpose of the project. "The Frazier family vision for the future – to revive a once vibrant neighborhood in order to create a true 'Beacon to the Community', right in the heart of North Philadelphia ... (while at the same time) bringing boxing back to its spiritual home." The package on the desk before Marvis also contained numerous drawings by artists, grandly depicting what the project might look like upon completion. Marvis was flabbergasted. Marvis was astounded. Marvis was sold! Here was everything he had imagined for the future of his dad's gym (and a whole lot more he hadn't even thought of!) all laid out before him in a format that made it appear perfectly feasible. These visitors really were angels, and this clearly was a miracle! As he sat at his desk in stunned amazement, all Marvis

Joe Frazier's gym as it is today. (Photo courtesy of Webster Riddick)

The gym as Marvis envisions it as "The Frazier Center"
(Reconstructed drawing by Ron Erwin)

could think to say was, "What do we do next?"

Over the next year and a half, the Joe Frazier Gym renovation project almost seemed to take on a life of its own, like so many large and varied projects do. The main role for Marvis was that of messenger. It was his job to get the word out and spread the "seeds" around wherever he could. This project was a huge undertaking, estimated at costing nearly ten million dollars, and would require the help of many people and organizations. Marvis took it upon himself to get as many of them on board as possible. First and foremost, of course, was the man whose name was on the masthead out front. Marvis had to tell his dad about his dream and get him to go along. That part of his job was easier than he expected. When Marvis met with Joe to share his plans, he told his dad about other businesses that had renovated their buildings. Then he began explaining his ideas for the gym, while placing the drawings on the desk in front of them. Joe was fine with the idea. He actually liked it, especially the part about the boxing museum, but Joe made sure Marvis knew that the money would have to come from sponsors or investors. What money he had would not be available. Joe ended the meeting with, "If you can get it together, Son, do it ... but you better hurry up."

Although Joe's last line sounded ominous, Marvis chose to focus on his dad's approval to go forward. He proceeded with near fanaticism. While his "angels" were busily pursuing the business end of the project, including financing, Marvis made copies of the plans, carried them around with him and showed them to every person who came through the doors. His persistence paid off when a board was created and several area professionals, who were also gym members, volunteered to participate.

Chapter 14 A New Dream

By the summer of 2007, everything seemed to be moving along nicely. The board of directors was in place and beginning to assume responsibility for much of the project. Sponsors were being signed up, and money was coming in. Marvis was still excited and trusting God daily through prayer that his dream for the gym would become a reality, but he was also starting to get nervous. "You'd better hurry up, Son." Joe offhandedly told Marvis one day in the gym, repeating his warning of a year earlier. Marvis knew what his dad was referring to. Unfortunately, even with huge renovation plans in the works, Joe Frazier's Gym was not very stable financially. Joe was warning Marvis that it might come down to a race between renovating the gym or closing it.

Over the next eight months, Marvis worked harder than ever on the renovation project, as well as the day to day operations of the gym. He wanted desperately to keep it open and continue to have a chance to see his dream come to fruition. Nevertheless, one day in March of 2008, his dad said they had to talk. They met in the office where so many important conversations had taken place over the years.

Joe spoke first.

"I'm tired, Son. I try to help everybody. Nobody helps me. Nobody worries about taking care of me."

"God will take care of us, Pop. You don't have to worry about all that."

"I've been taking care of people and nobody wants to take care of me."

"Pop, this is going to take care of you. It's going to be great ... and you know it will make money, (too)."

"Shut it down."

"(But) Pop, this is everything you stand for. Come on, Pop, we can do it."

"Nah, shut it down."

Joe Frazier's Gym was closed on Monday, March 30, 2008.

Marvis was devastated again.

Five years later, Marvis spoke about that conversation in an interview. "When Pop said, 'Shut it down,' it just killed me. I never asked for anything from my father. All I wanted was his love. That's all."

(Photo courtesy of Sadie Potter)

Chapter 15

Daddy Loves You

"I think fathers should take control of families. Those(children are) part of you. You brought (them into) this world. How (can) you not be a (good) father (to them)? How (can) you not be a good leader (for them)?" (Joe Frazier responding to a question about being a father in a 1986 interview on ABC Television Sports.)

      Marvis, remember when you were little and living at your old house on Ogontz Avenue? Remember playing "monster" with your father? He would lay on the living room floor while you and your sisters would try to sneak past the "sleeping" monster. Of course, you were never quiet enough to keep from waking the monster or fast enough to run past his out stretched arms. "I've got you now!" he would holler as he grabbed you and held you just long enough for you to cry out to your mother, who was most likely chuckling in the other room. "Help me, Mommy!" fell on deaf ears, but the monster would release you and fall back asleep, so you could get far enough away to try it all again. Your father never seemed to tire of the monster game. He was so much fun.
  Marvis, remember when you were a bit older, and your father would come home from a trip to Atlantic City. "Hey, you went to Atlantic City, Daddy?" and boom, a bunch of money would appear from inside his sports jacket. He'd say, "Let's play a little game right now." Your father taught you kids the game of "21," with real betting, and real money. It was fun to play and the best part was that

your father always made sure no matter who won, you each had some money when the game was over.

Speaking of money, Marvis, remember when you got your first job and you were earning money? Good money, too, a teenager in the mid 1970's earning $115.00 a week - $115.00 a week, living at home with no real expenses. You thought you were rich! You worked for Mr. Clark, who owned a cleaning company. Unfortunately, the job was a bit risky. Sometimes you had to crawl into ventilation ducts to clean them. Doing that made you congested, because you reacted to the dust it kicked up. Other times you had to hang by a belt hook from the walls of two story buildings in order to clean the windows. You didn't care much about those risks, after all, $115.00 a week! However, when your father found out what was going on, he had a different reaction. "What are you doing, Clarky, trying to kill my son?" Uh – uh, Marvis, you're not doing that, no way. You get down from there, right now." Your father was concerned about your safety so he wouldn't let you take those risks, but he also knew how much it meant for you to have a job and earn some money. Remember how he offered you a deal? "Marvis, how much is Clarky paying you? $115.00? Okay, I'll give you $150.00, and I'll make a list of what I want you to do." Remember all the jobs your father came up with? You had to start with cleaning and polishing all of his cars every week. That was a lot of work but at least you were safe, and you still got to learn about having some responsibilities.

Most of what your father did or said to you contained lessons of some kind. Remember the time your father took the whole family to Disneyland in California? As was always the case when you were out in public with your father, people flocked around him and tried to get his autograph. That time at Disneyland you were tired of all the fans and wanted your father all to yourself. After you had waited for what seemed like hours, there was only one little boy left to talk to your dad. You said, "No!" and shooed him away. Wow, was your father ever mad at you. He told you to run and find that little boy, apologize to him, and bring him back for an autograph. And do you remember what your father told you after the little boy left, with an autograph in hand? "Marvis," he said, "this is how Daddy makes his living. These fans put money in my pocket. They are the reason we can be here at Disneyland. And you are pushing them away? Don't ever do that again."

Some of the lessons you learned were hard to accept. Remember in early 1973 when your father fought George Foreman in Jamaica? You were only twelve years old, and you thought your father was indestructible, like the heroes in comic books. You were at ringside for the fight, wondering how quickly your dad was going to knockout Big George. Remember how surprised you were during the first round when Foreman knocked your father down? "Daddy, don't play man. Why are you playing? Stop that playing. Stop playing," You hollered out to your dad, laughing at his antics. Remember when your father went down again? "Daddy, stop playing man. Why are you playing? Why are you playing?!" You shouted to him, more seriously this time. And remember the third knock down? It was then that the reality hit you. "Daddy's not playing," you thought to yourself. Remember when the fight was over, less than one round later, and George Foreman was the new heavyweight champion? That was when you learned your father was human, just like any other man.

Remember just three years later in the Philippines, when you accompanied your father and his staff as they prepared for his third fight against Muhammad Ali? The fight came to be called the "Thrilla in Manila" and was your dad's last shot at regaining the heavyweight title. For you, though, the experience was what convinced you to become a boxer. Remember how your father allowed you to miss school for three weeks and then despite being busy training hard for the fight, he took the time to throw you a big bash for your fifteenth birthday party? Everyone was there including Philippine President Marcos and his wife, Imelda. The cake your father ordered for you was a huge thing and he had it topped with two sumo wrestler statues. It was so thoughtful of your father to do that for you.

That was some birthday celebration, but I know you'll never forget your sixteenth birthday either, because that was the year of "the Car." Remember how your dad flew off to Detroit for some reason, then a few days later came home with a new car? But it wasn't just any car. He already had some cool cars, but this one was one of the coolest. It was a 1976 Cadillac Seville. Remember, it was sky blue - inside and out. "The Car" had a Rolls Royce grill and half a hard top. The beautiful blue was offset by spoked mag wheels and white walled tires. "The Car" was a sight to behold, and when you first set eyes on it through the front window of the house; you bolted out the door to get a closer look. "Pop, you got a nice car. Dad, this is nice."

Remember how coy he was about it? "Yeah, you like it huh?" he asked you, then surprised you with, "Well, okay, well ... it's yours."

"Yeee Ha!"

"But," he warned you, "You had better keep it clean. If

Chapter 15   Daddy Loves You

I see one speck of dirt on it, I'm taking it back."

Of course, you kept it spotless because you were that kind of kid. You were still a kid then, but fast becoming a man. You had just gotten your driver's license, and you were just starting your amateur boxing career. Your father seemed happy that you wanted to be a boxer. Although he was very busy with his own careers as a boxer and a singer, he would still show up occasionally at your amateur matches.

Remember when you fought Tony Tubbs for the championship between the Joe Frazier team and the Muhammad Ali team? You were both undefeated, and the match was broadcast on television. Your father was there, and he was invited to help announce the fight. It was a great fight between two great amateur fighters, reminiscent really of a Joe Frazier/Muhammad Ali fight. Your father was enjoying working with fellow boxer, Ken Norton to help provide some expertise to the fight commentary. Everything went fine for about one round, but as the intensity increased going into the second round and then the third and final round, your dad could not contain himself. He left his announcer's seat (but kept his microphone), rushed up to the ringside and started cheering for his son! Remember how, when we listened to the tape of that fight years later, all we could hear near the end was your father shouting out instructions and Ken Norton laughing in support of a man whose love of his son temporarily trumped his stint as a TV announcer? Congratulations on a nice win in that fight, incidentally.

Marvis, remember how at your first professional fight in 1980, your father was in your corner for the first time? That night you celebrated your twentieth birthday and your first win as a pro. You were happy with the results, but your father didn't like the way the fight went. He promised to make changes and with that promise put into motion a union of teacher and student, between father and son, that would grow in strength and stand the test of time.

Remember your father as your trainer? He offered to you everything he knew about boxing, lined up your opponents, made you tough enough to continue your career even through the difficult emotional times, and helped you to make a living at a sport that you loved. Remember that your father was straight with you at the outset, never forced you to continue, gave numerous opportunities for you to say no, and did not argue with you when you finally did? Do you remember the breakfasts together before the big fights, the CB radios you both had ("This is 'K.O. One' calling 'K.O. Two'. You copy, 'K.O. Two'?") and the time you and your dad sparred for the sake of the photographer from Sports Illustrated magazine (You shouldn't have used the "Ali Shuffle")?

Remember after you retired and you became an ordained minister at the Faith Temple Church of God? Your father was just as proud of you then as he ever was for any of your boxing accomplishments. Remember how he attended your first ever service in the fall of 1994 and congratulated you in front of the congregation with a long emotional hug? From then on, your father would proudly tell people that you were a preacher ("just like George Foreman"), in the same way that you might tell people that your dad had been the heavyweight champion of the world.

Marvis, remember how you two worked together to run the gym? How you did your best to preserve it as one of the spiritual homes of boxing and at the same time address the spiritual needs of each person who came through its doors. Remember that even after those doors

Chapter 15 Daddy Loves You

closed, you and your father stayed together, traveling the country to make personal appearances and attend special events. While he was always the star of the show, you did whatever you could to keep that star shining. You were, after all, just returning a small portion to your father of all that your father had given to you.

November 25th, 1983 - Your fight with champion Larry Holmes is over.

"No man in the world could be any lower than I was at that moment ... "

{Smokin' Joe Frazier rushes to embrace his son}

"So, I was standing in the ring with tears coming down my cheeks, and I see my father coming through the ropes and walking toward me. I said, 'Pop, I messed up so bad.' But my father walked up to me. He had a big smile on his face, and his arms opened as wide as the world. He hugged me, and he said, "Don't worry, Son. I've got ya. You're my son, and I love you. Don't worry about what the world says, I love you."

Always remember Marvis, Daddy loves you

Smokin' Joe Frazier died November 7, 2011.

A short time later, writer and friend of Marvis, JoAnn Chmielowski penned these words about the loss of a father: "When I lost my father two years ago, I asked myself, "Where did he go?" The answer that came to me was clear. He is everywhere I am now. At this painful time, we are also privileged with joy - Joy, in awareness that a deep closeness with those we love who pass before us, is far greater than we had ever imagined. Take comfort in this closeness, as he is now with you everywhere you are.

"And I love my Dad"
(Photo courtesy of Webster Riddick)

Part V Hope

Rejoice in hope, be patient in tribulation, be constant in prayer.
Romans 12:12 (from the New Testament of the Bible, English
Standard Version)

(Photo courtesy of Webster Riddick)

Chapter 16

Marvis Frazier Today: A Conversation

And we know that all things work together for good to them that love God, to them who are the called according to his purpose. (From the King James Version of the New Testament: Romans Chapter 8:28)

Jamie: How are you today, Marvis?

Marvis: Blessed by the best, trying to share with the rest.

Jamie: Marvis, you've often told me that your life has been an incredible journey. The road has not always been easy. Let's start at one of the biggest bumps in that road, a pivotal point in your life, the fight with Larry Holmes in 1983 for the heavyweight championship of the world.

Marvis: Bring it on!

Jamie: When your former trainer, Sam Hickman, told you that you weren't ready to face Larry Holmes several months before the fight, how did you respond to him?

Marvis: "No way in the world, Sam. What are you talking about? I'm ready to go." I had no doubt in my mind.

Jamie: Did you ever talk to Sam Hickman about his prediction after the fight?

Marvis: Yes, the next time I saw Sam, he opened his eyes wide and said, "I told you."

Jamie: Had Sam ever suggested that you weren't ready for any of your other opponents?

Marvis: He felt that I wasn't ready for my amateur fight with "Bonecrusher" Smith, but I won that fight.

Jamie: Were you two life long friends?

Marvis: Yes. Unfortunately though, Sam is now deceased.

Jamie: You have been criticized for dropping your gloves during that short lived match with Larry Holmes. Did you ever do that against other opponents?

Marvis: Yeah, I did that with almost all my opponents, before and after Larry Holmes. Larry knew he was missing me, and if you miss your opponent long enough, he'll make you pay for it.

Jamie: You thought of yourself as a warrior. Explain what you meant by that?

Chapter 16 Marvis Frazier Today: A Conversation

<u>Marvis:</u> As a boxer, you train and you condition yourself to get into the best shape of your life. I had done that for Larry, and I had no doubt that I was going to win, until I got hit with that right hand!

<u>Jamie:</u> What if you had become the heavyweight champion of the world? What kind of champion would you have been?

<u>Marvis:</u> I would have been the same guy that I am. I would have taken on all comers. I would have tried to consolidate the titles just like Tyson ended up doing.

<u>Jamie:</u> After Larry Holmes knocked you down, you went right back at him. What were you thinking?

<u>Marvis:</u> I was a warrior. I thought, "Okay, I'm getting this guy back for that."

<u>Jamie:</u> With about twenty seconds to go, Larry Holmes trapped you in the corner and you couldn't get out. Was that a matter of inexperience?

<u>Marvis:</u> I had always been able to get out of the corner by moving to my right or punching my way out. The reason I couldn't get out with Larry was because he had tagged me.

<u>Jamie:</u> The scene at the end of that fight, when your dad came into the ring to console you, must be one of the most touching displays of affection in boxing history. You have used that story in your personal testimony as an analogy to show God's love for His children. Can you explain that analogy?

Marvis: You don't know how low I felt. It was like I didn't lock the doors of the house and just let the enemy come in and take everything. It was the lowest point in my life, and my father didn't turn his back on me, just like God doesn't turn His back on His children. He will never leave nor forsake them.

Jamie: Are you friends with Larry Holmes now, and is there a rematch planned in the near future?

Marvis: Larry and I are definitely friends. When we get together we always kid about a rematch. We decided they're gonna have to give us some more pennies though.

Jamie: As a youngster, you were a really nice kid, polite, respectful, and responsible. You were a peacemaker. Some critics claim that, for those very reasons, you could never have been the top boxer in the world. How do you respond to that criticism?

Marvis: You can tell that to all the guys I beat to win all those amateur titles. You can be competitive without being a brute. To me, boxing was a skill that you learned.

Jamie: You have a special place in your heart for South Carolina. Tell me about that.

Marvis: I was born in Beaufort County, South Carolina, and I loved it there because that's where many of my relatives were. We went back there every summer and stayed at the three hundred sixty-five acre plantation that my dad bought for his mother.

Chapter 16 Marvis Frazier Today: A Conversation

Jamie: Tell me the story about your father cutting up his Olympic Gold Medal.

Marvis: Pop wanted to do something special with his Olympic Medal, so he cut it up into eleven pieces, one for each of his children. He also had a diamond set in each piece, and a chain attached.

Jamie: We know that you excelled in several sports in school before you limited yourself to boxing. Did you have a favorite among the other sports?

Marvis: Yes, I played almost all the sports, but I loved football the most. I was a fullback, and I could run everyone over. I thought I was gonna be the next Jim Brown.

Jamie: In 1975, you went to the Philippines with your dad for his third fight with Muhammad Ali. What was your favorite part of that trip?

Marvis: There were many memorable moments on that trip and it's hard to pick one favorite, but I really enjoyed going to the airport when Mr. Ali arrived and singing *First Round Knockout* to him.

Jamie: That fight was, by far, the one Mr. Ali hyped the most. His behavior seemed to have deeply wounded your father. What were your father's feelings toward his arch rival later in his life?

Marvis: In later years, Mr. Ali came to Philadelphia and visited my dad in his apartment. They hugged and they said, "Let's let all this stuff go."

Jamie: Do you think your dad's wounds ever completely healed?

Marvis: I can remember going to a event called "The Great Ones" where Pop and Mr. Ali were getting awards. In the hallway of the hotel we spotted Mr. Ali sitting alone. He was shaking. Pop just started crying and said, "Look at that great man. Where are all the people now? Where are all his friends?" Then my dad just broke down.

Jamie: Before the last round of the third fight between your dad and Muhammad Ali, your father's trainer, Eddie Futch, stopped the fight, overruling the pleas from your father to let it continue. How did you feel about that decision?

Marvis: The trainer is the boss, and I thought Mr. Futch made the right decision. He loved my dad and had seen a few men die in the ring. He didn't want that to happen to Joe Frazier.

Jamie: As an amateur you had three great trainers. Of the three, Val Colbert stayed with Frazier's gym for his entire career. Are you still in contact with Val?

Marvis: Val is a great friend of mine. He was at every one of my fights. I see Val often when I go to Philly. I either stop off at his home and visit with Val and his wife, Elaine, or he and I meet for lunch.

Jamie: As an amateur, you won your first forty-four fights in a row over a four year period. What was it like for a young man to win every time?   Did it go to your head?

Chapter 16   Marvis Frazier Today: A Conversation   203

<u>Marvis:</u> It wasn't a problem for me. All of those wins just made me more confident. As an amateur, I trained hard, and I never missed a day in the gym.

<u>Jamie:</u> Your amateur career ended sadly with an unfortunate loss to James Broad in the Olympic trials. Do you remember how you felt at that time? How did you deal with the disappointment?

<u>Marvis:</u> I felt bad. I just knew I was going to get that medal and to lose, because of that fluke injury, didn't seem to make sense to me. I just had to suck it up, man. You have to learn that when you go into the ring anything can happen.

<u>Jamie:</u> You said that one of the best things about your amateur career was that it gave you the opportunity to travel the world. What did you mean by that?

<u>Marvis:</u> There's no place like home! When you see how other people live, and see the poverty, it makes you realize how lucky we are in this country. Seeing that changed my life.

<u>Jamie:</u> At the end of your amateur career, did you have any doubts about going on to become a professional?

<u>Marvis:</u> At the time, I didn't understand why I lost in the Olympic trials, but I felt that God had given me all this talent. Why wouldn't He want me to use it? So I decided to turn professional and see what happens.

<u>Jamie:</u> Your first four professional fights were fought at

Madison Square Garden. How did it feel to be fighting in the place where so many great boxers fought?

Marvis: I thought, "Man, this is so awesome to be here." Then, when I stepped into the ring I thought, "Yeah, this is the big time now."

Jamie: When you won your first professional fight you were happy about it, but your father wasn't. He made changes that eventually resulted in George Benton leaving Frazier's gym. All these years later, what do you think about losing George as one of your trainers?

Marvis: Nobody knew, at the time, that the rough start in my first fight was because of the same neck injury that caused me to lose in the Olympic trials, so my dad thought maybe George Benton was the wrong guy to train me. However, George was a great trainer, and he really knew his stuff. He was the right guy for me. I wish he could have stayed.

Jamie: You were undefeated when you fought Larry Holmes for the heavyweight championship, but you had only ten professional fights. Your former amateur trainer, Sam Hickman, said it was too soon to take on Larry Holmes. Now, thirty years later, after a lot of time to think about that loss, what do you think?

Marvis: Sam was right. I was just pig-headed.

Jamie: One of the most amazing things about your career is that after you lost to Larry Holmes, you fought and won six consecutive fights while in the throes of depression. How did you do it?

Marvis: I have to attribute that to the Lord. I wasn't "there" emotionally, but I just followed the routines that I always followed.

Jamie: The majority of your fights were against boxers who were bigger than you. That never seemed to be a problem. Why not?

Marvis: I was absolutely confident I was going to get the job done. Those guys were tall, but I could reach their chins. I know they could reach mine, too, but I was going to make them miss.

Jamie: Since you were twenty years old you have carried with you a long, thick scar on the back of your neck. Is it your badge of courage or just a reminder of how close you came to serious, long term injury?

Marvis: I never gave it too much thought. The injury was fixed. That's all I ever thought about it.

Jamie: Your surgeon, Dr. Simeone, tried to talk you out of continuing the sport of boxing. What did you think of his suggestion at the time?

Marvis: I felt that the Lord wouldn't bring me this far to stop now, especially since we knew what the problem was and it had been fixed.

Jamie: Dr. Simeone has stated that in this day and age, a doctor would not release an athlete to continue a contact sport after undergoing the type of surgery he performed on you.

What do you think about that?

Marvis: I think it should be the athlete's choice. I would never sue a person for a decision I made. You cannot blame other people for choices you make.

Jamie: Did you know that when Dr. Simeone took out the bone that protects your spinal chord in the back of your neck, he didn't replace it with anything, since the muscles and tendons in that area are enough protection, even for a boxer?

Marvis: Oh, man! So that's the reason Mike and Larry beat me!

Jamie: In your mind, did your fight with Mike Tyson have the same level of importance as your fight with Larry Holmes?

Marvis: Oh, the Holmes fight was much more important. The fight with Larry was a championship bout, but the Tyson fight was only a chance to get back to a championship fight.

Jamie: Usually, when lists of the all-time greatest heavyweight boxers are made, Larry Holmes and Mike Tyson are ranked in the top ten, or even the top five. Since you fought them both, where would you rank them?

Marvis: One and two!

Jamie: After seeing how quickly Mike Tyson knocked you out, there are people who say that you have a glass jaw, or can't take a punch. How do you respond to that?

Chapter 16   Marvis Frazier Today: A Conversation

Marvis: I'd tell them to look at my record and see who I fought before they make that judgment. Do all of the champions who Mike Tyson knocked out have glass jaws?

Jamie: How do you think Mike Tyson, in his prime, would have fared against other great fighters in boxing history: Joe Louis, Rocky Marciano, George Foreman, or even your dad?

Marvis: It's hard to speculate about fights between boxers from different eras. Though I know Pop would have taken him out... but I'm prejudiced on that one!

Jamie: Before the fight with Larry Homes you said you were on cloud nine. What cloud were you on after you lost that fight?

Marvis: Cloud zero!

Jamie: That loss was the beginning of your depression. The morning after the fight you woke up feeling like you were in a deep hole. Did it ever occur to you that you would be stuck in that hole for five years?

Marvis: It never crossed my mind. I thought I was just going through something I didn't understand. I kept telling myself that I would feel better tomorrow.

Jamie: For quite awhile you tried to keep your feelings of depression to yourself. Why?

Marvis: I didn't understand what depression was. I figured that since it had just come upon me it would just go away.

Jamie: How did Daralyn deal with your depression?

Marvis: Daralyn was very compassionate. She would say, "Honey, you'll be alright. It'll come together."

Jamie: Explain the phrase "How am I doing, Pop?" and how it related to your depression.

Marvis: Normally a boxer knows exactly where he stands in a match. During my depression, even when I was winning, I couldn't tell and needed reassurance from my dad.

Jamie: It's interesting that upon retiring from boxing you immediately felt the depression lift. How do you explain this?

Marvis: It was a miracle. All I had to do was follow God's plan for my life and the healing took place.

Jamie: After the depression disappeared you became your happy-go-lucky self again. What is the happy-go-lucky Marvis Frazier like?

Marvis: Happy and lucky. Life is so happy with me and I am so happy with life.

Jamie: Speaking about happy and lucky, tell me about your family.

Marvis: My daughters, Tamyra and Tiara, are doing well. They both live with their families in the Philadelphia area. They've blessed me with seven smart, beautiful grandchildren: Tamyra has one boy and one girl, and Tiara

Chapter 16 Marvis Frazier Today: A Conversation

has three girls and two boys. I love to talk to my grands on the phone and visit them whenever I can.

Jamie: By the late 2000's you had a wonderful dream for the renovation of your dad's gym. Unfortunately, it didn't work out at that time. If the gym renovation had worked out, what would you be doing today?

Marvis: I'd still be at the gym, and I'd be the happiest man in the world! I'd be making sure everything was in its proper place, everything was running smoothly. I'd probably be working twenty hours a day, but hey, that's cool. I'd be happy greeting visitors at the door. "Welcome to Joe Frazier's Gym!"

Jamie: Do you believe there could still be a miracle ahead for the gym, and that your dream of renovating it is still a possibility?

Marvis: Yes, it's always a possibility. With God all things are possible. The building is still there.

Jamie: What if someone reading this book contacted you and said, "Let's buy the gym back and build your dream." Would you do it?

Marvis: Oh man, Yeah!

Jamie: You said that if everyone had a father like Joe Frazier this would be a lot better world. What did you mean by that?

Marvis: My father always said, "There is no right way to do wrong and no wrong way to do right, so do right." If people were more like my dad, this would be a more caring, generous, loving world. And I feel the same way about my mom, the "sweet lady" Florence Frazier.

"Pop, I messed up so bad."
"Don't worry, Son. I've got ya."
"How am I doing, Pop?"
"You're doing good. You're wining the fight."

(Photo courtesy of Webster Riddick)

Afterword

What Meeting Marvis Frazier has Meant to Me
By Jamie Potter (March 6, 2013)

When I first called the number for Joe Frazier's Gym in the summer of 2009, I had a mental image of Marvis Frazier answering the phone. I had never met Marvis Frazier, but had seen him in the documentary *Thrilla in Manila*, sitting at his desk in the office of the gym giving an interview. As I dialed the number I imagined Marvis sitting at that same desk, picking up the phone to receive my call. Little did I know that Joe Frazier's Gym had closed about a year before, and when Marvis answered he was speaking from a makeshift office in his dad's apartment.

"Hello, this is Jamie Potter calling from upstate New York, I'm calling for Marvis Frazier."

I was actually calling for Joe Frazier but I figured my chances were nearly zero that *the* Joe Frazier would answer my call; probably it would be a secretary and maybe he or she could put me through to Marvis (On later calls, actually intended for Marvis, I often did get *the* Joe Frazier. He would say hello, kid around a bit, then pass the phone to his son).

"This is he." came a reply from a voice that sounded a lot like the man in the documentary.

I was caught off guard but tried to calmly continue the conversation, thinking to myself – I'm talking to Joe Frazier's Son! The exchange was made remarkably easy by the pleasant nature of the man on the other end of the line. Marvis was extremely personable as well as funny. Of course, I was interested in him, but he seemed interested in me too. We talked for about five minutes during which time I expressed my desire to see his father in person.

I explained that I hauled Pennsylvania peaches during the summer and suggested that perhaps I could meet them sometime while I was in the Philadelphia area. Marvis ended up calling me Jamie "The Peach Man" Potter, and told me he was sure it could be arranged.

Over three years have passed since that fateful phone call. As I think back, I realize that at the time I had no idea the future would find us working together on a book about his life, but somehow, I think I did know that someday he and I would become the best of friends.

(Photo courtesy of Sadie Potter)

Appendix 1

"Young Christian"

Many years ago they brought us all here by ships.

They separated us from our mommas and daddies, they beat us with whips.

We became defeated, we almost lost our minds,

but a still small voice said, "Young Christian, it's praying time."

I dropped to my knees and cried, "Man, what have I done?"

"Be still young Christian, you're a chosen one."

I said, "Lord, this cup is much much too hard for me to bear.

Why was I not called to be another man instead?"

He said, "Hold it young Christian and let me tell you what will become of you,

if you continue trusting me and to your own self be true.

Out of your loins will come prophets, priests, rulers, and kings.

So yes young Christian, I expect much from you,

especially when they mock and laugh and spit at you too.

They will mock you, they will slap you,

they will beat you to the ground.

But young Christian, when this world seems to have gotten the best of you,

open your Bible, yes, I'm in there, you see, I am a young Christian too."

- *Marvis Frazier*

(Photo courtesy of Webster Riddick)

Appendix 2

Marvis Frazier's Professional Record

19 Wins (8 knockouts, 11 decisions), 2 Losses (2 knockouts)

Result	Record	Opponent	Type	Rd., Tme	Date	Location
Win	19-2	Philipp Brown	Decision (unanimous)	10	10/12/88	Tucson, Arizona
Win	18-2	Robert Evans	Decision (unanimous)	10	08/10/87	Secaucus, New Jersey
Win	17-2	Tom Fischer	TKO	2 (10), 2:47	06/01/87	Secaucus, New Jersey
Loss	16-2	Mike Tyson	KO	1 (10), 0:30	07/26/86	Glens Falls, New York
Win	16-1	James Smith	Decision (unanimous)	10	02/23/86	Richmond, California
Win	15-1	Jose Ribalta	Decision (majority)	10	09/11/85	Atlantic City, New Jersey
Win	14-1	James Tillis	Decision (unanimous)	10	05/20/85	Reno, Nevada
Win	13-1	Funso Banjo	Decision	10	12/05/84	London, UK
Win	12-1	Bernard Benton	Decision (unanimous)	10	10/23/84	Atlantic City, New Jersey
Win	11-1	David Starkey	TKO	1 (8), 2:50	09/25/84	Pennsauken, New Jersey
Loss	10-1	Larry Holmes	TKO	1 (10), 2:57	11/25/83	Las Vegas, Nevada
Win	10-0	Joe Bugner	Decision (unanimous)	10	06/04/83	Atlantic City, New Jersey

Result	Record	Opponent	Type	Rd., Tme	Date	Location
Win	9-0	James Broad	Decision (unanimous)	10	04/10/83	Atlantic City, New Jersey
Win	8-0	Mike Cohen	KO	2	03/07/83	Charleston, South Carolina
Win	7-0	Amos Haynes	TKO	5 (10), 2:23	02/08/83	Atlantic City, New Jersey
Win	6-0	Guy Casale	Retirement	4 (8), 3:00	09/16/81	Las Vegas, Nevada
Win	5-0	Tony Pulu	Decision (unanimous)	6	08/22/81	Las Vegas, Nevada
Win	4-0	Steve Zouski	TKO	6 (6), 2:13	05/11/81	New York, New York
Win	3-0	Melvin Epps	Decision (unanimous)	6	04/10/81	New York, New York
Win	2-0	Dennis Rivers	TKO	2 (4), 2:30	10/10/80	New York, New York
Win	1-0	Roger Troupe	TKO	3 (4), 2:08	09/12/80	New York, New York

Amateur Awards

Marvis Frazier had an amazing amateur boxing career. Over a five year period he averaged one match per month for a total of fifty-eight fights with fifty-six wins and only two losses. Marvis started out by winning his first forty-four matches in a row before finally losing in a close decision to Tony Tubbs. During his five years as an amateur, he defeated nearly every top heavyweight amateur in the country including: Jimmy Clark, Mitch Green, Tony Tubbs, Philipp Brown, James "Bonecrusher" Smith, and Tim Witherspoon. With those kinds of credentials it is not suprising that Marvis won a host of amateur titles and awards. The list includes:

Three years as the Pennsylvania Golden Gloves Heavyweight Champion
1979 National Golden Gloves Heavyweight Champion
Ohio State Fair National Heavyweight Champion
(Also named Most Outstanding Boxer)
1979 Junior Olympic World Heavyweight Champion
(Also names Most Outstanding Boxer)
1980 United States Amateur (AAU) Heavyweight Champion

Appendix 3

Book Writing Outtakes: A Blog Post Record of Our Journey

Sometimes, if you stay long enough at the end of a movie in the theater, you get to see extra clips of the movie known as outtakes. These edited segments are often funny or give you an inside look at what went into the making of the film. Likewise, if you keep reading far enough beyond the main story of this book you get to see our "book writing outtakes," which are a collection of blog posts from the Meet Marvis Frazier website. We can't say for sure that they are funny (although we tried!), but they will give you an inside look at some of what went into the making of this book.

Thanks, Jamie

Marvis and I began work on the book back in the fall of 2009. We started out slowly, but made steady progress. Still, after about two years there was a lot left to do. Then Marvis lost his dad and work on the book came to a grinding halt. About four months passed and then:

Marvis Frazier Book Project is Back on Track

Posted on February 21, 2012

After some unfortunate delays, the book about Marvis Frazier's life is back on track. Nearly everyone knows that Marvis's Dad Smokin' Joe Frazier passed away November 7th – and naturally Marvis was deeply affected, but about the time Marvis and I were re-starting our interview work for "the book," my own Dad became gravely ill. James Walter Potter, Sr., who I consider a great man, a great father, and a great athlete in his own right, died on January 31st, 2012. So now, partly from a desire to "move on" and partly in a effort to honor our Dads, Marvis and I are going back to work on "the book" and we are going to kick it right into high gear – after all the launch date is only a little over one year away!

Joseph William Frazier *James Walter Potter*
(Photo courtesy of Webster *(Photo from family collection)*
Riddick)

Marvis only fought twenty-one times as a professional, but I kept daydreaming about all of the interesting fights he could have had. So, one time I daydreamed my way right into a blog post about it:

What if Marvis Frazier had Fought George Foreman?

Posted on March 4, 2012

Marvis Frazier's professional career lasted from 1980 until 1988 and included 21 fights. Of those 21 fights, several were against big name boxers, including of course, Larry Holmes and Mike Tyson, but also James Tillis, Joe Bugner, and "Bonecrusher" Smith. During the 1980's there were so many good fighters battling to get to the top of the heavyweight division. I can't help wondering how Marvis Frazier would have fared against some of them and why these match-ups never took place.

Two that immediately come to mind because of similarities in size and style with Marvis are: Michael Spinks and Evander Holyfield. Both were champions at other weight classes and then moved up to become heavyweight champs. Spinks beat Holmes but then like Marvis, was destroyed by Tyson. Holyfield had Tyson's number, beating him twice. How would Marvis Frazier have done against these two champions? I think they would have been great fights!

A few other fighters who won titles in the 80's seem like natural match-ups for Marvis but no such match-ups ever occurred. Tim Witherspoon and Tony Tubbs both held the title at one time or another during the 1980's and Marvis had beaten both in the amateur ranks. Why weren't professional bouts ever arranged? Pinklon Thomas, who won the WBC heavyweight title in 1984 was a bit older than Marvis and they never met in the amateur ranks, but they sparred at Joe Frazier's gym frequently. Wouldn't a title match between those two "buddies" have been a super fight?

Finally, since George Foreman, the only fighter, other than Ali to beat Marvis' Dad, Smokin' Joe (twice), started his amazing comeback in 1987, while Marvis was still fighting, what if Marvis Frazier had fought George Foreman? Since George was older and slower would Marvis have been able to revenge his Dad's two losses to the big guy? Come to think of it, Larry Holmes retired in early 1988 after losing to Mike Tyson. Maybe he could have been lured out of retirement again by a not so young or inexperienced Marvis Frazier anxious to erase an important loss early in his career. Now that would have been an interesting fight!

I often joke with Marvis about him becoming a vegan. Then while doing research on Mike Tyson (Mike Who?) I discovered that Mike is a vegan. That gave me even more ammunition to use with Marvis:

Marvis Frazier, Mike Tyson, Veganism, and Me

Posted on March 17, 2012

Marvis and I just finished a chapter in our book about his experience fighting Mike Tyson in 1986. Of course to complete such a chapter I had to do a lot of research on "Iron Mike." During that research I discovered that

Mike Tyson is now a vegan and has been for a couple of years. A vegan is a person who abstains from the use of animal products, especially in their diet. I was surprised that Tyson practices veganism because the bravado he displayed during his fighting days conjured up the image of him running down animals in the woods, killing them with his bare hands, ripping the meat off their bones, and eating it raw! Yet in the interviews I watched of Mike on Youtube talking about his new diet, he mentioned the weight he has lost (150+ lbs.!), the disappearance of his joint pain, and his overall better health since he became a vegan. Mike also said that because of this sort of success, he was a vegan for life – there was no way he would ever give up veganism.

Ironically, I recently became a vegan myself. Of course if Mike Tyson had threatened me with "become a vegan or else ..." I wouldn't have challenged him with "or else, what?" – but my path to veganism was one of much less pressure than that. My wife Janet and I have been vegetarians since college days (a LONG time ago), but it was our wonderful son Jack who convinced us (and our daughter, Sadie) to throw out the dairy and eggs and get ALL the benefits of a plant based diet and some philosophical consistency too. That was about ten months ago and I have to agree with "Iron Mike" (who would dare to disagree with him?), we have never felt better! I would have to say that like Mike Tyson, we, too, are vegans for life.

Now, as for Marvis, I broached the subject with him a few weeks ago and told him about Mike. He was less than enthusiastic but mentioned how much he likes fruits and vegetables. I guess that's a start. I'd like to urge him a bit more, but I'm not about to try any strong arm tactics with a former heavyweight title contender like Marvis Frazier. However, my son Jack is 6' 4" and was a killer defenseman in his High School Ice Hockey playing days …

Jack (Photo from family collection)

I get a kick out of how far I have come in my understanding of boxing since those first interviews. Maybe you will too:

Marvis Frazier: the Early "Interviews"

Posted on March 30, 2012

The initial "interview" sessions that Marvis Frazier and I had were very informal, yet very informative. The first one was over the phone and for warm up chit chat we talked about my other (or some might say real) business, which is what I call agricultural entrepreneurship (farming ... my first book was a children's book about gardening). I explained to Marvis that during part of each summer I hauled peaches for a living. After that Marvis began calling me Jamie "The Peach Man" Potter and continued that nickname for some time. Now he only calls me that when I present him with some of those juicy fresh fruit delights. It turns out that peaches are one of Marvis Frazier's favorite foods.

Later, when we first met in person, I couldn't help showing my ignorance about the sport we both loved when I asked how one keeps from getting hit in the throat when boxing (I had participated in a "backyard" version of the sport as a teenager and when I challenged the best of the backyard boys, I thought my time on earth was finished when he punched me in the throat). Marvis laughed that wonderful laugh of his and answered simply, "keep your chin down" (why didn't I think of that?).

When our discussion got more to the point regarding his career, I asked Marvis how he felt about his fight against Mike Tyson (ouch!). To my pleasant surprise, Marvis replied without hesitation, "I wish I could fight him again!"

"Really?" I said. "How would you fight him differently?"

"I would move more, stay out of the corner, stick him and move."

Wow, that impressed me – as did many other things Marvis Frazier told me that day.

Finally, as our time together was drawing to a close, I asked him one more important question. "Marvis, what would you think of me writing a book about you?"

This time Marvis was the one who was surprised. "Really?" He said. "Why me?"

I've always enjoyed kidding around with Marvis about the two of us going at it in the ring – and believe me I mean kidding around. Here's a sample:

My Plan to Best Marvis Frazier (Think Bo Jackson)

Posted on April 5, 2012

Often, when I talk to Marvis Frazier, I'll kid around with him about how I've been working out lately and I'm finally ready to take him on, or I've been watching a lot of his fight tapes and I know his moves enough now to take him on, etc., etc. Of course Marvis just chuckles and doesn't even respond. Once I sent him a picture of me "boxing" my brother when I was about ten (just to scare him). That got a response. Marvis called and left a message for me. I knew it was Marvis because I know his laugh!

Anyway, I'm guessing that Marvis isn't worried about us ever being matched up in the ring. Maybe I should try a different sport. Well, I used to play baseball; how about we square off on the diamond. Then again Marvis was an excellent catcher in his baseball playing days. Hmmm? I played football too – a well under 200lb. offensive guard. Aaahhh, Marvis was a star running back on his football team. How about wrestling? I was a pretty good wrestler in school. What? Marvis was the wrestling champion in his school's region?!

By now you probably get the picture. I was an athlete, I played several different sports over the years. Marvis, on the other hand, was a star in every sport he played. He was kind of a Bo Jackson type. You know, great at every sport he ever tried ... almost.

So, here's my plan. Next winter (just about the time the book is done), when the ice is ready around here, I'm going to invite Marvis up for a little skating session; maybe we'll even play a bit of ice hockey. You see, as Wayne Gretzky once made clear to Bo Jackson in a TV commercial, no matter how great an athlete you are (Bo Jackson or Marvis Frazier), if you can't ice skate then you are going to suck at ice hockey. Marvis can't ice skate but I used to play ice hockey, so I know I'm going to get the best of him all over that ice.

Heck, if I can get his jersey up over his head while he's floundering around out there on the ice, I might even out-box Marvis Frazier that day too!

When I first met Marvis, he and his dad still had the gym, although it was closed. For a treat during one of my trips to Philadelphia, he took my daughter, Sadie and me over for a tour. One thing that struck me right away when I walked in there was the size of the boxing ring:

This Ring is WAY too Small!

Posted on April 15, 2012

I kid around a lot with Marvis Frazier about boxing with him, but believe me I have never suffered from the illusion that I would stand a chance in the same ring with Marvis or any other pugilist – and I felt that way even before I ever stepped into a ring. A boxing ring is not a big place. The size of the ring does vary, ranging from 16' by 16' (amateur minimum) to a maximum professional size of 25' by 25', with most professional rings being 20' by 20'.

Now you might think that sounds big, but a good way to dispel that thinking is to get into one. A few months after Marvis and I started the book about his life, he invited my daughter, Sadie, and me to Philadelphia for dinner. While we were there, Marvis took us downtown to visit his Dad's Gym. It was exciting just to be heading toward Joe Frazier's Gym, but stepping inside the door of the place was like a fantasy. Despite being closed and showing signs of age, the gym was still set up like it had been during its hay day when so many of the greatest in the sport put in regular appearances. The creaky wooden floors, the walls – covered with pictures of the greats, the various punching bags suspended from the ceiling, and the Ring. Right there in the center of the room was the same ring where Smokin' Joe, Marvis, and so many other great boxers had fine tuned their skills.

Appendix 3 Book Writing Outtakes

My daughter Sadie, being an amateur photographer of sorts was drawn by all the pictures on the walls, but I was mesmerized by that Ring. I just had to get up into it. So I checked with Marvis then jumped up on the skirt, slipped through the ropes, and was in. Wow! I spun around to look at each of the four corners. It was just an empty boxing ring but my imagination quickly filled it with all the details of fight night: the lights, the crowd, the press, the referee, and the ring announcer. And yes, I was suddenly much younger and in my first professional fight! My opponent? Why not? I was fighting Big George Foreman.

Just about the moment my imagination placed the 6'4" 250 lb. giant in the opposite corner of the ring I was gripped by a spell breaking realization; this ring is WAY too small!

You know ... I like playing ice hockey; 60' by 200' sheet of ice and lots of room to run when the big guys are after you. I also admire Marvis Frazier more than ever after being in that little 20' by 20' space.

Sadie with Marvis in that small ring. (Photo courtesy of Sadie Potter)

You should know by now from reading this book that Marvis is a very thoughtful human being. In case you somehow missed that message, here is more of it for you:

Marvis Won the Golden Gloves of Giving

Posted on May 8, 2012

I have mentioned before in these blog posts and it is discussed in the book that Marvis Frazier was an excellent all around athlete. He excelled in: Baseball, Football, Basketball, Wrestling, and of course, Boxing. His performance in these sports as a junior high school student did not go unnoticed by the high school coaches at Plymouth-Whitemarsh, where he would be attending beginning in his freshman year. Several of the coaches had scouted Marvis and were already making plans for him to come on board with their teams.

Imagine their disappointment when they found out that Marvis would not be available. Once Marvis made it clear to his Dad that he was serious about pursuing boxing, his Dad made it clear to Marvis that he needed to dedicate himself to boxing; all the other sports would have to go. Marvis capitulated to his Dad's wishes but felt badly about giving up the other sports. Marvis enjoyed all the sports that he played and because he excelled at them, he knew that he could have contributed to the success of the school sports teams he would have played on.

Some of the coaches tried to convince Marvis and Joe to let Marvis compete on their teams, but to no avail. From age 16 on, Marvis was a boxer exclusively. Of course Marvis did succeed at his chosen sport. Even while he was still a student at Plymouth-Whitemarsh, Marvis won the 1979 National Golden Gloves tournament, winning himself a title and ... well, a golden glove.

Sometime after winning that glove, Marvis was again feeling badly for not playing other sports for his high school teams, when he got an idea. There was an upcoming sports award assembly and Marvis asked the school athletic director if he could speak briefly. Of course this already nationally famous and very popular student could say a few words.

Part way through the assembly, Marvis was called to the podium on the stage. He calmly addressed his fellow students, congratulating them on their athletic successes during that school year. Marvis then apologized for not being out there on the field with the others to help them achieve even greater success. "As a consolation for my absence," he told the entire student body, "I would like to offer my golden glove as a trophy to represent all the students at Plymouth-Whitemarsh High School."

Throughout the country, hundreds of high schools have trophies for league, section, or state championships in one sport or another, but how many have a trophy with laces for a championship of the entire nation? Then again, how many high schools have had a student win the Golden Gloves of Boxing and the "Golden Gloves of Giving?"

The following post became the most popular on our website blog. I guess a lot of people discuss the topic it covers. Marvis is only mentioned twice in passing but my old friend from high school, Keith Day, who is the main character, became a mini sensation on the internet because of this post:

Is Boxing the Most Physically Demanding Sport?

Posted on May 17, 2012

When I was growing up in a small town in upstate New York, most of the boys in my group of friends played a number of different sports, but there was this one guy who outdid us all. "Keith," who was a real good athlete, played all the usual sports like baseball, football, basketball, along with soccer, wrestling, and ice hockey. Keith, however, was the only guy in our group who also participated in amateur boxing. Very impressive, especially considering that Keith had to travel to the nearest city to do so. Another thing that impressed me about it was when Keith told me that of all the sports he ever tried (see above list), boxing was by far the most strenuous.

I had to think about that for a while. After all, I had played most of the other sports in Keith's sports resume and some of them were quite taxing. All the boxing I had ever done was the back yard version; you know the kind where two guys lace on gloves somebody got for Christmas and start wildly swinging at each other until the bigger guy finally knocks the other guy senseless and then the next two guys in line take their turns. But I had wrestled and those wrestling practices were grueling, especially if you had to make weight and the temperature was turned way up in the practice room. How about those double practice sessions at the beginning of football season? Although once you were in shape and started hitting, that's when the fun began. Basketball: now there's a "non-contact" sport that can really take it out of ya'. Up and down, up and down, up and down the court, hustle, hustle, hustle. If you're covering on defense you have to hustle in basketball. Not too bad on the bench though. Soccer is a running game and that soccer field is a big one, but you do have ten other players to pass off to or help you play defense, so … Ice hockey? Sorry, sheer joy for me. Finally, baseball. There's nothing more fun than taking batting practice in baseball and fielding practice isn't too bad either.

I guess "Keith" was probably right about Boxing being the most physically demanding of the traditional American sports. I suppose it has to do with the whole business of punching and being punched. I only wish I knew a real boxer who I could ask about it {Marvis Frazier}, you know, someone who played a lot of other sports, too {Marvis Frazier} … "jah well" (as the Amish used to say).

Hey, did I say that I used to be a bowler? Talk about your physically demanding sports!

Okay, so sometimes I couldn't think of anything to write about when it was time to write a blog post and ended up pulling a subject right off the top of my head, but the last line in this post cracks me up:

What's Your Favorite Boxing Movie?

Posted on July 4, 2012

So sorry for the long dry spell at the blog watering post. Suffice it to say that I've had a few things going on. About a month ago, not long after my last post, I had an idea for this post and though it coulda, shoulda, woulda been posted in early June, I guess I'll give it a try now.

Movies about boxing. You see them all the time. I'm kind of a movie buff (owned a video rental place on the side for a few years), and I can think of dozens of titles, but just about anyone can think of at least six – you know, *Rocky one, two, three, four, five, and six*. There are all kinds. Movies with boxing as the main theme like *Rocky one, two*, etc., *The Champ*, or *Raging Bull*. And movies where boxing is a part of the setting for some other theme to be played out, like *On the Waterfront* with Marlon Brando, and *The Boxer* with Daniel Day Lewis. There are dramatized versions of famous boxer's lives like *The Great White Hope* (Jack Johnson) and *Somebody Up There Likes Me* (Rocky Graziano), then there are straight up documentaries like *When We Were Kings* and *Thrilla in Manila*. There are even comedies about boxing like Barbara Streisand's *The Main Event* and *The Prize Fighter* with Don Knotts and Tim Conway.

As it is with movies in general, since there are so many boxing movies to choose from, it is hard to pick a single favorite. I guess I'll take the easy way out and talk about four of my favorites.

I'll start with *Rocky* (the original). Boy did Sylvester Stallone hit it out of the park with this movie. Stallone, who wrote the picture and starred in it was virtually unknown before this 1976 sports classic won the Academy Award for Best Picture. The simple story was nonetheless filled with memorable lines. My two favorites were when Burgess Meredith as Rocky's trainer tells the going nowhere young fighter that being a debt collector for gangsters is "not a living, it's a WASTE of LIFE!", and when the fight between Rocky and Apollo Creed is over, Creed shouts to Rocky over the noise of the crowd "There's not going to be a rematch!", to which Rocky replies "Don't want one!" (but there will be 2nd, 3rd, 4th, 5th, and 6th movies).

Next there is *Raging Bull*. Martin Scorsese's depiction of the life of boxer Jake LaMotta is brilliant and Robert De Niro is incredible in the title role (also winning the Academy Award for his performance). Leave it to Scorsese and crew to provide a depressing yet magnificent version of the dying american dream through this great film (and leave it to the geniuses of *Waiting for Guffman* to parody its lines for their own comical purposes).

A third boxing movie that really moves me is *Requiem for a Heavyweight*. This movie written by *Twilight Zone* creator Rod Serling in the late 1950's, was initially made for TV, then rolled out by Hollywood with the likes of Jackie Gleason, Anthony Quinn, Mickey Rooney, and Julie Harris starring. It is an incredibly dramatic story and the acting is top notch. It has also been performed on stage over the years. Watch it if you ever get a chance.

Finally I want to talk about the boxing documentary *Thrilla in Manila*, starring none other than my main Man

Marvis Frazier (oh, and his Dad Smokin' Joe Frazier, Muhammad Ali, Larry Holmes, etc.). This is a wonderful documentary about the amazing third fight between Frazier and Ali – some say the most brutal fight of all time. I happened upon it a few years ago through a review of it in the newspaper, but that minor event became major in my life after I met Marvis Frazier because of it. And now you know the rest of the story … or if you don't you will when our book comes out!

PS. What is Marvis's favorite boxing movie? He's not saying right now. He wants to reserve judgment until he sees who will be playing him in the movie based on our book (not really, I just made that up —Marvis doesn't care who plays him in the movie!).

This is a nice little story that will give you a bit of the amazing history behind Marvis and I coming together to write the book about his life:

"Why You, Marvis Frazier?" "Why Me, Jamie Potter?"

Posted on September 3, 2012

After filling my 1983 Dodge truck with gas, I completed my routine of buying the *USA Today* newspaper. I had no intention of reading the paper at that time, after all it was already 10:30 and I was expected at the peach depot by noon, but by buying it now I would have it when I stopped for lunch or supper later. Eventually, after reaching my destination on time, loading the peaches, and heading back north, I did stop for lunch and I did read the paper.

Most of the news of the day was of no interest to me, but as I leafed through, passing over the "national news," "business," and "sports" sections, something caught my eye in the "living" section. There on the page that listed the new releases on DVD was a review of a movie I thought I would enjoy. It was a documentary about the rivalry between boxers Joe Frazier and Muhammad Ali. It was entitled *Thrilla in Manila*, named I presume after their third and final fight. What piqued my interest was the indication that the film focused on Joe Frazier. I finished my sandwich, made a mental note of the release date, tossed the newspaper into the can with the rest of my trash, and headed back to the truck.

As the release date of the movie approached, its unavailability at the local Blockbuster led me to order my own copy directly from Amazon. On the day of its arrival in the mail, I decided that I would start to watch it that night. In the same way that there are books you can't put down, *Thrilla in Manila* was a movie I could not stop watching. Even though I was thoroughly tired from a long day of physical labor in my farm fields and should have turned in at my usual bedtime, I stayed locked on this story and its real life characters. Although I thought of myself as a big fan of the 1970's boxing era, the Joe Frazier/Muhammad Ali rivalry was much more dramatic, much more compelling, much more captivating than I ever imagined ... and the saga included several fascinating characters I was barely aware of.

One such person in the film was Marvis Frazier. Marvis, the son of Smokin' Joe, held a ring side seat at the career of his father, especially during the Frazier/Ali fight trilogy when Marvis was a teenager. Marvis even had a fine boxing career of his own. This much about Marvis Frazier I knew or surmised. What I did not know about Marvis is a course regarding the human heart that could fill an entire book.

Midway through the movie, Marvis tells the story of witnessing the end of his father's undefeated streak at the hands of George Foreman. Hearing his emotional revelation that this was the first time he realized that "My dad was human just like any other man," had me fighting to keep my own emotions in check. Near the end of the DVD, when Marvis described his dad's wonderfully supportive reaction to his own heartbreaking loss during a shot at the title against champion Larry Holmes, I was wiping tears from my own eyes as Marvis was there on the screen wiping them from his.

A few weeks later when through a series of remarkable events, my daughter and I were on our way to meet the Fraziers in Philadelphia, I was as excited to meet Marvis Frazier as I was to meet his world famous father.

Since that fateful first watching of the documentary; a handshake, a face to face conversation, and numerous phone calls have only served to reinforce my writer's intuition that Marvis Frazier has a story to be told and that I am the one who should tell it.

Why you, Marvis Frazier? Son of the great Smokin' Joe Frazier, excellent boxer in your own right, preacher of the gospel, man who has many stories to tell. Why me, Jamie Potter? Small business owner, jack-of-all-trades, full time farmer, part time writer. Because, Marvis, after all that has happened in such a short period of time, I believe, maybe, destiny wants it that way.

PS. This essay/short story was written one week before Marvis and I got together to discuss the writing of the book about his life and was presented to him at that meeting.

Appendix 3   *Book Writing Outtakes*   237

And here's some of the story of what happened after we got together:

Is It a Book Yet? What Does He Do Around Here, Anyway?

Posted on October 10, 2012

About half way through the audio greeting from Marvis on the home page of our website, you can hear Marvis say "I have a book coming out, Jamie has been working on it for I don't know how long." Marvis, who takes what life hands him in stride, doesn't keep track of such things and doesn't worry about them either. Me, on the other hand, I'm just a little bit more uptight about deadlines (even if they are self-imposed) and I can tell you exactly how long we have been working on the book (more about that later). After all, I look at that count down clock everyday when I open the e-mails to the website and if nothing else it reminds me just how fast time flies (when you are having fun or writing a book!). 141 days?

So here's the math: Marvis and I started the book two years and eleven months ago, almost to the day. It took us nearly four months of interviews and conversations before the first word was put to paper, then enough additional words poured out to give us the rough draft to chapter one (you can hear a reading of it on the home page). Individual chapters were slow to come but an outline for the entire book was finished after about a year's time and hasn't needed much adjustment since. The interviews and conversations we have had, if written down verbatim, would fill volumes. But just as the maple sap collector boils away so much water to get to the syrup, the writer has to strain a sea of words to get to the story. "Straining" for this book has been easy because the story is so great and so easy to see. 141 days?

So, after two years and eleven months, almost to the day, the text of the book is nearly done. Hallelujah! But, because the story is almost done, is it a book yet? Well, even setting the entire publishing part of the process aside, here are a few of the things that still have to be done: copy editing (good grammar please), fact checking (was that really what he said?), photo selection (aww, Marvis, you were so cute when you were a kid), cover design (that ought to get your attention), foreword ("and the mystery foreword writer is … "), afterword (by yours truly), credits page (expert witnesses), back cover design (that ought to keep your attention), acknowledgments page (thanks Mom, Dad, Sis …), table of contents (that's in there?), index (that word is in there … twice?), etc. (and so on). 141 days?

Thinking of all that Marvis and I have done so far on the book, yet all we still have to do somehow reminds me of the time a new employee at our store kept making suggestions to my son of things I could do to help the two of them close the store quicker. My son, knowing I had a huge list of "owner" things to do myself, kept telling the new employee "No, my dad can't help us with that." Finally, after about ten of his work suggestions for me were vetoed by my son, the exasperated but naive new employee barked out "well, what does he do around here, anyway?!" 141 days!

Appendix 3   Book Writing Outtakes   239

Here is a post that gives more information about what Marvis did after he retired from boxing. If I really had been a boxer, I would have liked having Marvis Frazier as my trainer! How about you?:

Marvis Takes a Turn (or Two) as Teacher and Trainer

Posted on November 10, 2012

"Why do we sacrifice?" "Because when you give something up something will come back!" (the 6th item of the "Creed of Joe Frazier's Gym," posted in the gym by Marvis Frazier) Like many athletes who excel at a particular sport, Marvis Frazier turned out to be an excellent teacher and trainer in that sport. Benefiting from having been taught by great trainers himself and immersed in the sport throughout his life, Marvis also has a magnetic personality and loves working with people. These factors, combined with great opportunities made Marvis a natural as a boxing teacher and trainer.

Even before his own retirement, Marvis was already helping his dad at the gym. Joe had a stable of young fighters he was trying to make champions and Marvis pitched right in to help. Having been in "the show" himself was more than enough to qualify him to contribute and advice, but Marvis also had a friendly way to instill confidence in the fighters he worked with. Marvis was like a big brother to the fighters, one they trusted and admired. After retirement Marvis put even more time and energy into the gym, including more training. He added lessons for life to the typical training, trying to turn out better boxers and better people. Along with the "Creed of Joe Frazier's Gym," Marvis incorporated "Ten Power Punches For Life" and "Rules For Respect" as important parts of participating at his Dad's gym.

As for training and teaching boxing outside of his Dad's gym, Marvis got a taste of that too. During the 1990's Marvis was invited by his friend and former trainer, Sam Hickman to work with the United States Olympic boxers. In this capacity, Marvis was available for the fighters at the Olympic center and traveled with the team for tournaments throughout the world prior to the Olympic Games themselves. One of the highlights of his work with the team was a tournament in Italy where the US boxers did very well and everyone got lots of free spaghetti and meatballs!

About a decade later, Marvis had another stint as a trainer outside of his Dad's gym when he worked with his own sister, Jacqui Frazier-Lyde. Jacqui was only two years younger than Marvis but in 2000, at the age of 38, she decided to take a shot at women's professional boxing. Luckily for her she had a world champion father, a very talented brother, and the fighting spirit of both. For the first two years of her three year career, Marvis taught Jacqui every thing he knew, helping her to a thirteen and one career record and two light heavyweight titles. I'm sure the brother and sister team had lots of fun working together those two years, but I can't help wondering if Jacqui ever got the opportunity to get Marvis back for the time he punched her in the stomach when they were kids!

As a teacher and trainer, Marvis Frazier proved himself to be a natural throughout the years, resulting in a high rate of success for "Power Punch 4" of the "Ten Power Punches For Life" that Marvis posted in his Dad's gym: Faithfulness Between Teacher & Student!

I've met a lot of nice, helpful people while Marvis and I have been working together on this book. One of the nicest, hands down, was Reggie Bullock. How could I not write a blog post about him?:

Let Us be Forward about the Foreword

Posted on December 19, 2012

Every good book needs a great foreword. The title and front cover may get the potential reader to pick up a book and even open it up to see more, but the foreword is the first textual material that is likely to be read and often helps to determine if the potential reader reads on — or even buys the book! With that in mind Marvis and I have thought long and hard about who we would like to write the foreword for our book about Marvis's life. Naturally, we realized the marketing advantages of having a famous celebrity do the honors and for that reason we communicated with some of the biggest names in the boxing profession. But Marvis and I also wanted a unity of message in the book from cover to cover so we kept an eye out for someone who not only knew Marvis Frazier, but understood him as well.

Of course, because the clock was running down and the publication date was getting closer, the pressure was on to pick someone from our list of candidates and close the deal. Then, like with so many other aspects of this book project, fate intervened and the problem of who to write the foreword nearly solved itself.

It all started when Marvis was interviewed on Blog

Talk Radio in October of this year. I was able to listen to the interview live but missed the first few minutes trying to get the connection right. It was an excellent interview that lasted nearly an hour. A few days later I was listening to a replay and was able to hear the show in its entirety, including the introduction of Marvis by the talk show host. Wow, I thought, this guy really "gets it" about Marvis Frazier!

And that was when it dawned on me. I immediately called Marvis to get his opinion. "Marvis" I said as I cued up a recording for him over the telephone, "listen to the introduction of you from the radio interview you did the other day — I think we have found the person to write the foreword for the book."

Fortunately for me, Marvis agreed; and fortunately for us both, radio personality and YouTube video maker sensation, Reggie Bullock, the man who interviewed Marvis that night and introduced him as though he had known him for life, agreed to write the foreword for our book. Along with being a radio personality, Reggie is an educator, public speaker, and filmmaker. His videos have been viewed by millions on YouTube. Reggie is bright, articulate, funny, and he loves Marvis! Like I said before, this guy "gets it" about Marvis Frazier and with Reggie Bullock writing the foreword, we are more likely to "get it" right in the book about Marvis Frazier's life. It'll be a book soon!

PS. Another piece of the project puzzle put in place by providence. (Hemingway probably would have hated that sentence)

The next thing you know Marvis and I will have jobs at Microsoft! Read on and see what I mean:

Facing Up to Facebook

Posted on February 1, 2013

People have said that Marvis and I both act younger than we are. However, we're old fogies when it comes to computers. Keep in mind: we are old enough to remember the excitement of watching Saturday morning cartoons (and I'm talking old cartoons, like Huckleberry Hound and Deputy Dog) on the fancy, "new" color TV, we both used to watch our school football films using a projector and a screen, and when we first rented videos in our 20's, we took the video machine home too. So when personal computers came along it was a giant technological leap for us both. Not that we each didn't see the benefits of computers; Marvis recognized their advantages in the operation of a business and welcomed the use of computers to help with office work at his father's gym. I saw how much the internet accommodated doing research and the word processor facilitated writing, so I too incorporated computers into my daily activities.

I guess the part of the information age that we have been slow to adopt is the social network aspect. Sure, we have this website. We need a presence on the web and a website is like a home, almost like a piece of property. From this "home" on the web we can get the message out about Marvis and his book to those searching the internet. We can use posts on our blog (like this one!) to keep people informed about the book and eventually set up a page to sell it once it becomes available (can anyone say

98 days?). But that ought to do it, a website is all we need.

Fortunately for us, our good friend Reggie Bullock (who wrote the foreword to the book) went through the same thought pattern we did about the social network aspect of the information age and survived to tell about it. "I know just what you are thinking," I remember him saying to me not long ago, "but my daughter convinced me that I had to get on Facebook to help publicize my film making and radio show, and it became the best promotional thing I ever did – you and Marvis need it too" Strong advice from a man whose opinion we don't take lightly.

So, Marvis and I mulled it over. Marvis and I talked it over. And Marvis and I turned it over – a new leaf that is, Marvis and I turned over a new leaf, bit the bullet, swallowed our pride, threw caution to the wind, and got Meet Marvis Frazier on Facebook! Surprise: five days in and it's fun, and it's exciting, and it's working. Thank you Reggie Bullock for convincing us. Thank you Sadie for helping us (you didn't think we could do it ourselves, did you?). And thank you all for going to Meet Marvis Frazier/facebook and "liking" us. To get there could hardly be easier, here's the link: http://www.facebook.com/meetmarvisfrazier. Or you can just Google: Meet Marvis Frazier/facebook.

Now, about that Twitter thing ...

PS. There are a couple of "Marvis Frazier" Facebook pages out there besides ours, but only the Meet Marvis Frazier Facebook page is authorized by "the Man" (Marvis).

If you're still here, Thanks for staying with us right to the bitter end. Where would we be without you? Still hauling Pennsylvania peaches for a living, I guess. Come to think of it, I am still hauling Pennsylvania peaches for a living! Marvis doesn't mind though, he loves peaches. You can leave the theater now.

Thanks much,   Jamie Potter and Marvis Frazier

*Marvis Kirk Frazier AKA Santa Claus
(Photo courtesy of Webster Riddick)*

Our Photographers

Webster Riddick with his son Webster and his daughter Mariah.

Darryl Lee, Sr.
Find out more about Mr. Lee by visiting his website:
www.mrleesphotofinish.com

INDEX

"Ali Shuffle" 87, 192
A.A.U. (Amateur Athletic Union) 20, 52, 114
ABC TV (ABC Sports) 106, 187
Academy Award 233
Achilles tendon 97-98
Albert, Marv 20, 67
Ali, Muhammad (Ali, "Mr. Ali") 9, 35, 37-42, 45, 47, 58, 74, 80, 82, 104, 116, 127, 146, 190-191, 201, 202, 220, 233-234
Andrew (Boyhood friend of Marvis) 145, 155 (photo:160)
Banjo, Funso 88, 133
Bartlett, Jenny 7
Battle, Rudy 88
Benard (Cousin of Marvis) 146-149, (photo:117)
Benton, Bernard 87, 133
Benton, George (George, Georgie) 40, 46-49, 51-52, 57, 61, 86, 204
Blog Talk Radio 242
Book of Job 174, 179
Boxer, The (Movie) 232
Boxing Hall of Fame 46
Brando, Marlon 232
Brandon (Brother of Marvis) (photo:121)
Broad, James (James "Broad Axe" Broad) 20, 53, 55-56, 59, 62, 71-73, 89, 99, 106, 128, 157, 203
Brown, Bundini 47
Brown, Jim 201
Brown, Philipp 63, 114-115, 141
Bugner, Joe 20, 73-75, 77, 129, 157, 219

Bullock, Isaiah 10-11, (photo:11)
Bullock, Reggie 7, 10-11, 241-242, 244, (photo:11)
Cadillac Seville 146, 151, 190, (photo:117)
Caesar's Palace 19-20, 66-67, 77
Carter, Rubin "Hurricane" 46
Casale, Guy 66-68
CBS Sports (CBS Sports Sunday, CBS Television) 32, 72, 74, 89
Chambers, John Graham 93
Champ, The (Movie) 232
Chmielowski, JoAnn 7, 194
Clancy Gil (Clancy) 72-75, 89-90
Clark, Jimmy 20, 54
Clark, Obe (Pastor Clark) 150-152
Cloverlay (Cloverlay, Inc.) 44-45
Cobb, Randall Tex 81
Cohen, Mike 70
Colbert, Val (Vellen Colbert, Val) 7, 31-32, 46-49, 51-52, 57, 59, 61, 109-110, 113, 137-139, 202, (photos:118, 136)
Colson, Chuck 108
Condon, John 60-61
Conway, Tim 232
Cooney, Gerry 64, 82
Cooper, Bert 83
Cooper, Henry 74
Cortez, Joe 62, 107
Creed of Joe Frazier's Gym 261
Creed, Apollo 233
Curtis, Joey 88
D'Amato, Cus 104, 128
Daralyn (Daralyn Evon Lucas, Daralyn Frazier) 21, 56, 75-79, 110-111, 115-116, 129, 131, 133, 135, 137-139,

141-142, 144-145, 147-169, 173-178, 208, (photos:76, 144, 160)
Day, George "Doc" 7
Day, Keith 230-231
De Niro, Robert 233
Deputy Dog 243
Derek (Brother of Marvis) (photo:121)
detached retina 95-96
Disneyland 78, 188-189
Douglas, James "Buster" 87, 161
Elaine Wallace-Colbert (Elaine) 7, 47, 202
Ellis, Jimmy 37, 74
Enon Tabernacle Baptist Church 176
Epps, Melvin 62-63
Erwin, Ron 7
Evans, Robert 113, 140
Fabiani, Dr. Joseph 8, 63, 93-94, 97-98, 100
Faith Temple (Church of God) 161, 163-164, 176, 192
Felt Forum 58-59, 61-62, 64-65
Fight of the Century 37, 58
First Round Knockout (Song) 38, 201
Fischer, Tom 112-113, 140
Foley, Brian 8
Foreman, George 32, 37, 65, 82, 104, 189, 192, 207, 219-220, 227, 236
Frazier Center, The 7, 182, (drawing:183)
Frazier, Florence (Smith, Florence) 5, 21, 33, 43-44, 50, 150, 163, 210, (photos:6, 120)
Frazier, Jacqui (Jacqui, Jacquelyn, Jacqui Frazier-Lyde) 33-34, 36, 44, 84-85, 146-150, 240, (photos:120-122)
Frazier, Jo-Netta 34, (photo:120)
Frazier, Joe (Joe, Smokin' Joe, Poppa Joe) 5, 9, 20-21, 28, 31-49, 51, 55, 57-61, 64-65, 70, 74, 77, 79-80, 84-87,

90-91, 93, 97, 100, 104, 107, 109, 112, 114, 116, 127, 129, 132, 134, 142, 146, 155-156, 163, 177, 183-184, 187, 191, 193, 202, 209, 211, 217, 220, 226, 228, 234-236, 239, (photos:6, 118, 120, 122-124, 185, 194, 218)

Frazier, Natasha 34, (photos:118, 120)

Frazier, Rodney (Cousin of Marvis) 82, 90, 114, (photos:117, 121)

Frazier, Weatta 34, 36, (photo:120)

Fried, Jack 35

Futch, Eddie 41, 202

Gideon 114

Glass, Sam 31-32

Gleason, Jackie 233

Glens Falls Civic Center 106

Golden Gloves 20, 51-52, 228-229

Graham, Billy 65

Graziano, Rocky 232

Great White Hope, The (Movie) 232

Greater Harvest Church 155

Green, Mitch (Big Mitch Green, Mitch "Blood" Green) 20, 54, 56, 63, 99, 106

Gretzky, Wayne 225

Hagler, Marvin 48, 82

Halpern, Bobby 66

Harris, Julie 233

Haynes, Amos 67, 69-70

Hearns, Thomas 67

Hemingway 242

Hickman, Sam (Sam) 19, 45-46, 48-52, 57, 77-78, 198, 204, 240, (photo:118)

Holmes, Larry (Larry) 9, 19-28, 31-32, 43, 45, 55, 67, 75-83, 87-91, 104, 106, 112, 116, 129-134, 138, 140, 156-157, 161, 173, 193, 197-200, 204, 206-207, 219-220, 234,

236, (photos:29-30)
   Holyfield, Evander 46, 219
   Howard University 154
   Huber, Hans 34
   Huckleberry Hound 243
   Hull, Chuck 19, 55
   Ingraham, Shirley (Potter) 6, (photo:6)
   It's a Wonderful Life (Movie) 35
   Jackson, Bo 224-225
   Jacobs, Jim 104
   Jet Magazine 77
   Job (of the Old Testament) 160, 174-175
   Joe Frazier's Gym 20, 44-45, 48-49, 57, 77, 81, 83, 86, 89, 111, 176-177, 179, 182-185, 202, 204, 209, 211, 220, 226, 239-240, 243, (photos:178, 183, drawing 183)
   Johnson, "Scrap Iron" 40
   Johnson, Jack 232
   Knotts, Don 232
   Kool & The Gang 116
   Kubler-Ross, Elisabeth 143
   laminectomy 101, (photo:102)
   LaMotta, Jake 233
   Lampley, Jim 105
   Lane, Mills 21-22, 24, 26-28, 78-79, 88
   Lee, Darryl 8, (photo:246)
   Lcifer, Neil 32
   Leonard, Sugar Ray 64, 67, 72
   Lewis, Daniel Day 232
   Lewis, Jerry 147
   Lewis, Lennox 63
   Lorin, Dr. Al 125
   Louis, Joe 207
   Lyle, Ron 74, 82

Madison Square Garden 57-62, 64-66, 204
Main Event, The (Movie) 232
Marciano, Rocky 19-20, 32, 66, 77, 80, 83, 91, 207
Marcos (Philippines president and his wife Imelda) 38, 190
Mark (Cousin of Marvis) 78, (photo:121)
Mathis, Buster 35
Mayisela, Steven 8
McCabe, Kevin 114
McCoy, Van 38
Medina, Joey "The Kid" 114-115
Merchant, Larry 64
Meredith, Burgess 233
Monroe, Willie "The Worm" 48, 82
Morrison, Tommy 65
NBC Network 20
New Jersey Boxing Hall of Fame 66-67
North Broad Street 179-180
North Philadelphia 179, 182
Norton, Ken 45, 64, 81-82, 191
O'Neil, Joe 70
Old Testament 113-114, 160, 174, 179
Olympic trials 52, 55, 59, 62, 71, 99, 100, 106, 128, 173, 203-204
On the Waterfront (Movie) 232
Order Blanks 258, 260, 262
Pacheco, Ferdie 20
Patterson, Floyd 49
Pennsylvania Hospital 166, 169
Pennsylvania peaches 212, 245
Philadelphia Bulletin 35
Plainfield Correctional Facility 107-108
Plymouth-Whitemarsh High school (Whitemarsh,

Whitemarsh High School) 154, 228-229
   Potter, Jack 8, 221, 222, (photo:222)
   Potter, James Walter, Sr. (Jim Potter) 5, 218, (photos:6, 218)
   Potter, Sadie 8, 221, 226-227, 244, (photo:227)
   Povich, Maury 127
   Powers, Janet 8, 221
   Prison Fellowship 108, 141, 161-162, 164-165, 167, 175-176
   Prize Fighter, The (Movie) 232
   Psalms 30:5 142
   Pulu, Tony 65-66
   Qawi, Dwight Muhammad 83
   Quarry, Jerry 37
   Quinn, Anthony 233
   Raging Bull (Movie) 232-233
   Rainone, Vincent 112
   Raising Arizona (Movie) 81
   Renae (Sister of Marvis) (photo:121)
   Requiem for a Heavyweight (Movie) 233
   Resorts International 71
   Ribalta, Jose 65, 88-89, 105, 133-134
   Riddick, Webster 4, 8, (photo with his children:246)
   Rivers (Brother of Marvis) (photo:121)
   Rivers, Dennis 61-62
   Rocky (Movie) 33, 232-233
   Romans 12:12 195
   Romans 6:23 151
   Romans 8:28 197
   Romeo, Dr. Donald 67
   Rooney, Kevin 104
   Rooney, Mickey 233
   Rules For Respect 257

Ryan, Tim 72-74, 89-90
Samson 113
Sands Casino Hotel 73
Scamboogah 85
Scorsese, Martin 233
Serling, Rod 233
Sharnik, Mort 32
Shavers, Earnie 74, 81-82
Showboat Casino 65
Simeone, Dr. Frederick 8, 63, 100-102, 205-206
Singleton, Charlie 50
Smith, James "Bonecrusher" 54, 83, 89-91, 105-106, 134, 137-138, 198, 219
Smokin' Joe and the Knockouts 47
Smokin' Joe Frazier Revue, The 47
Snipes, Renaldo 63
Somebody Up There Likes Me (Movie) 232
Spinal Congenital Stenosis 101, 128
Spinks, Leon (Leon) 46, 83
Spinks, Michael 83, 90-91, 94, 219
Sports Illustrated (Magazine) 65, 86, 192
Stallone, Sylvester 233
Starkey, David 87, 133
Stinson, Marvin 81
Streisand, Barbara 232
Tamyra (Marvis's oldest daughter) 131, 158, 161-162, 167, 173-176, 208-209, (photos:118, 172)
Temple University 179
Ten Power Punches For Life 259
Thomas, Pinklon 81, 97, 219
Thrilla in Manila (The actual fight and the documentary) 38, 40, 178, 190, 211, 232-233, 235-236
Tiara (Marvis's youngest daughter) 140, 158, 161,

167, 173-174, 176, 208-209, (photos:118, 172)
   Tillis, James (James "Cowboy" Tillis) 74, 88, 105-106, 133-134, 219
   Tolle, Eckhart 171
   torn retina 95
   Triplett, Dwight 82
   Tropicana Hotel and Casino 67
   Troupe, Roger 59-61
   Tubbs, Tony 20, 50, 54, 65, 89, 191, 219
   Twilight Zone 233
   Tyrone ("Cousin" of Marvis) (photo:121)
   Tyson, Mike 32, 65, 88, 103-113, 115, 128, 135, 140, 159, 161, 173, 199, 206-207, 219-221
   Uncommon Valor (Movie) 81
   United States Olympic Team 52, 240
   USA Today 234
   vegan 220-221
   Waiting for Guffman (Movie) 233
   Wallau, Alex 105
   Walsh, Joe 47
   Wayans, Keenan 78
   WBA (World Boxing Association) 35, 80, 83
   WBC (World Boxing Council) 19, 71, 81, 87-89, 97, 104-105, 112, 140, 219
   When We Were Kings (Documentary) 232
   Williams, Carl "The Truth" 82, 87
   Witherspoon, Tim 20, 54, 82, 89, 156-157, 219
   World Football League 58-59
   Wyncote 131, 158, 162, 176
   Yemelayanov, Vadim 34
   Young, Jimmy 46, 62, 82, 100, 114
   Zouski, Steve 64-65

RULES FOR RESPECT

RESPECT GOD

RESPECT PARENTS

RESPECT BROTHERS & SISTERS

RESPECT OTHERS

RESPECT SELF

(Posted at Joe Frazier's Gym by Marvis Frazier)

Ordering Information

If you enjoyed this opportunity to Meet Marvis Frazier and would like to order additional copies of the book, check for availability with a local bookstore, an online bookseller, or place an order directly using information on this order form. Thank you.

For Online ordering: Go to – MeetMarvisFrazier.com

For Telephone ordering: Dial – 607 643 7212

For Postal Ordering: Use a copy of this form and send a check or money order in US funds to:
>Gopher Graphics
>3883 State Hwy. 7
>Otego, New York 13825

Name:_____

Address:_____

City:_____ State: _____

Country:_____ Zip or Postal Code: _____

Telephone:_____

E-mail address: (not required, but helpful)_____

Pricing

Book Price:	$24.95
Shipping and Handling:	+ 7.05
Total Cost:	$32.00

NYS orders + $2.00 Sales Tax = $34.00 Total
International orders, additional $13.00 S&H = $45 Total

Optional:	Book Autographed by Marvis Frazier	+ $10.00
	Book Autographed by Jamie Potter	+ $7.00
	Book Autographed by Both	+ $15.00

Pricing, Shipping & Handling, and Sales Tax requirements are subject to change

Contact us at: meetmarvisfrazier@hotmail.com or
gophergraphics@hotmail.com

TEN POWER PUNCHES FOR LIFE

POWER PUNCH 1.
EDUCATION IS POWER!

POWER PUNCH 2.
ALWAYS BE OBEDIENT TO YOUR PARENTS!

POWER PUNCH 3.
LOYALTY TO YOUR GYM AND COACHES!

POWER PUNCH 4.
FAITHFULNESS BETWEEN TEACHER & STUDENT!

POWER PUNCH 5.
WINNERS NEVER QUIT AND QUITTERS NEVER WIN!

POWER PUNCH 6.
GIVE RESPECT TO YOUR ELDERS!

POWER PUNCH 7.
FAITHFULNESS & COOPERATION BETWEEN BROTHERS & SISTERS!

POWER PUNCH 8.
FAITHFULNESS BETWEEN FRIENDS!

POWER PUNCH 9.
GET THE JOB DONE!

POWER PUNCH 10.
LIFE IS A CHALLENGE AND WE'RE GOING TO BEAT IT!

(Posted at Joe Frazier's Gym by Marvis Frazier)

Ordering Information

If you enjoyed this opportunity to Meet Marvis Frazier and would like to order additional copies of the book, check for availability with a local bookstore, an online bookseller, or place an order directly using information on this order form. Thank you.

For Online ordering: Go to – MeetMarvisFrazier.com

For Telephone ordering: Dial – 607 643 7212

For Postal Ordering: Use a copy of this form and send a check or money order in US funds to:
Gopher Graphics
3883 State Hwy. 7
Otego, New York 13825

Name:_____
Address:_____
City:_____ State: _____
Country:_____ Zip or Postal Code: _____
Telephone:_____
E-mail address: (not required, but helpful)_____

Pricing

Book Price:	$24.95
Shipping and Handling:	+ 7.05
Total Cost:	$32.00

NYS orders + $2.00 Sales Tax = $34.00 Total
International orders, additional $13.00 S&H = $45 Total

Optional:	Book Autographed by Marvis Frazier	+ $10.00
Book Autographed by Jamie Potter	+ $7.00
Book Autographed by Both	+ $15.00

Pricing, Shipping & Handling, and Sales Tax requirements are subject to change

Contact us at: meetmarvisfrazier@hotmail.com or
gophergraphics@hotmail.com

CREED OF JOE FRAZIER'S GYM

WHO'S THE BEST?
WE'RE THE BEST!

WHO'S THE BEST TEAM?
WE'RE THE BEST TEAM!

WHY ARE WE THE BEST?
BECAUSE WE WORK HARD!

WHY ARE WE THE BEST?
BECAUSE WE SACRIFICE!

WHY DO WE WORK HARD?
BECAUSE WE'RE DISCIPLINED!

WHY DO WE SACRIFICE?
BECAUSE WHEN YOU GIVE SOMETHING UP,
SOMETHING WILL COME BACK!

WHY ARE WE DISCIPLINED?
BECAUSE WITHOUT DISIPLINE
THERE IS NOTHING!

(Posted at Joe Frazier's Gym by Marvis Frazier)

Ordering Information

If you enjoyed this opportunity to Meet Marvis Frazier and would like to order additional copies of the book, check for availability with a local bookstore, an online bookseller, or place an order directly using information on this order form. Thank you.

For Online ordering: Go to – MeetMarvisFrazier.com

For Telephone ordering: Dial – 607 643 7212

For Postal Ordering: Use a copy of this form and send a check or money order in US funds to:
Gopher Graphics
3883 State Hwy. 7
Otego, New York 13825

Name:_____
Address:_____
City:_____ State: _____
Country:_____ Zip or Postal Code: _____
Telephone:_____
E-mail address: (not required, but helpful)_____

Pricing

Book Price: $24.95
Shipping and Handling: + 7.05
Total Cost: $32.00

NYS orders + $2.00 Sales Tax = $34.00 Total
International orders, additional $13.00 S&H = $45 Total

Optional: Book Autographed by Marvis Frazier + $10.00
Book Autographed by Jamie Potter + $7.00
Book Autographed by Both + $15.00

Pricing, Shipping & Handling, and Sales Tax requirements are subject to change

Contact us at: meetmarvisfrazier@hotmail.com or
gophergraphics@hotmail.com